# Confronting the Silence
A Holocaust Survivor's Search for God

ALSO BY WALTER ZIFFER

*The Teaching of Disdain: An Examination of Christology and New Testament Attitudes Toward Jews* (1990)

*The Birth of Christianity from the Matrix of Judaism* (2006)

# Confronting the Silence
## A Holocaust Survivor's Search for God

by Walter Ziffer

DYKEMAN
LEGACY
PRESS

Copyright © 2017 by Walter Ziffer

All rights reserved. Except for brief passages in critical articles or reviews, no part of the book may be used or reproduced in any manner whatsoever, including information storage and retrieval systems, without prior written permission from the publisher.

Published by Dykeman Legacy Press, a division of Wilma Dykeman Legacy, Inc.
60 Shuford Road, Weaverville NC 28787
www.wilmadykemanlegacy.org

Book design by 828:design, Asheville, NC
Map design by Creative Force Inc., Tampa, FL

Photo credits: unless otherwise credited, cover and interior photographs provided by the author from his family album.

Front cover quote: Michael Sartisky, PhD
President Emeritus, Louisiana Endowment for the Humanities

Printed in the United States of America.

ISBN: 978-0-9975269-0-5

Library of Congress Control Number: 2016956934

10 9 8 7 6 5 4 3

*This memoir is dedicated to
the three most important women of my life:
Anny, the lovely woman who co-produced me into life;
Carolyn, with whom I lovingly co-produced and
co-nurtured our four children; and
Gail, who makes my life sweet every day.*

Northeastern Europe, showing the location of Walter Ziffer's hometown Český Těšín

# CONTENTS

Map: Northeastern Europe, showing the location of Walter Ziffer's hometown Český Těšín
Preface to the first version of the memoir .......................... 1
Preface to this version of the memoir ............................. 3
Photographic section ........................................ 119-122

**PART ONE: MY EARLY YEARS**

    Chapter 1: My first prayer ........................................ 7
    Chapter 2: First tastes of antisemitism ....................... 13
    Chapter 3: Polish takeover ...................................... 25
Map: Locations of Nazi camps mentioned in this memoir......... 32

**PART TWO: IN THE CLUTCHES OF EVIL**

    Chapter 4: Here come the Nazis ............................... 35
    Chapter 5: My first love and tragedy ......................... 43
    Chapter 6: Initiation into hell: Sakrau ....................... 61
    Chapter 7: In the midst of hell: Brande ....................... 67
    Chapter 8: From Brande to Klettendorf ....................... 81
    Chapter 9: Schmiedeberg, Waldenburg and liberation ...... 91
    Chapter 10: Difficult return home ............................. 111
    Chapter 11: A new start in our hometown.................... 117
    Chapter 12: The chess game ................................... 133
    Chapter 13: Champigny-sur-Marne and Paris ............... 137

# CONTENTS (Continued)

**PART THREE: AMERICA**

Introduction .................................................... 145
Chapter 14: Nashville, Tennessee ............................. 147
    American high school
    Encounter with the Jewish community of Nashville
    Vanderbilt University and Carolyn
    Inland Equipment Company, graduation,
        and on to Dayton, Ohio
Chapter 15: Gibsonburg, Ohio and Graduate School
    of Theology ................................................ 159
    Graduate School of Theology at Oberlin College
    Professor H.G. May and Marie
Chapter 16: Le Chambon and Montpellier, France ......... 167
Chapter 17: Washington, DC ................................... 175
Chapter 18: Brussels, Belgium ................................. 179
Chapter 19: Nova Scotia, Canada ............................. 187
Chapter 20: Return to the USA: Bangor, Maine and ......... 193
    Weaverville, North Carolina

**EPILOGUE: NEW HORIZONS** .................................... 209

Biographical timeline for Walter Ziffer ..................... 216
For further reading............................................. 219
Discussion questions .......................................... 220
The Wilma Dykeman Legacy.................................... 221

# Preface to the first version of the memoir

The Jewish people have an old custom of writing so-called ethical wills. Very often it is parents who leave this document for their children in which they try to sum up the important lessons life has taught them. They also may use this document to express what they most want for and from their children. Just as parents leave behind some of their material possessions to their children, so ethical wills bequeath to them a bit of the wisdom they may have acquired during their lives.

It is not easy to write an ethical will. In doing so, one must introspect. One must confront oneself as objectively as possible. This means that one has to face up to one's failures and also try to determine what it is that really counts in life. In writing an ethical will honestly, the person learns about himself or herself and then lays her or his soul bare before the reader.

Sometimes an ethical will is not easy to read. In it information may surface that the reader may not want to know because it demolishes previously held ideas about the writer which are hard to give up.

So let me hasten to say that this is not an ethical will. This is a memoir and in that sense it is more like a diary than ethical instruction. On the other hand, it is not impossible to imagine that the reader of these pages may be able to find some new and interesting insight here.

I have tried to relate the major events and developments of my life on a chronological basis, interspersed at times with remembrances or insights that sporadically came to mind as I wrote. If these confuse, I apologize.

If the present version of this memoir reads considerably better than the first draft I prepared, it is thanks to my wife Gail's corrections and suggestions to make the document more readable. I am deeply grateful to her for her efforts to improve the work.

It is most regrettable to me that my sister Edith, *z"l* (may her memory be a blessing), 1923 – 2001, is no longer around to read this memoir and to give me general feedback. After I left my homeland in 1947, hundreds of letters were exchanged between my parents and me. When my mother and father became old and could no longer handle the correspondence, it was Edith who continued exchanging letters with her younger brother on a regular basis. I admired Edith very much for her love, uprightness and tenacity. She hated the Nazis for what they had done and never held back expressing it. Edith could have left Czechoslovakia just as I did and for all that I know, she may have been tempted to do so. But her love for and loyalty to our parents prevented her from leaving them. When my father and later my mother died, she was at their side when they needed her most, while I was far away in America. Edith was a lovely human being.

And so I dedicate this memoir in Edith's remembrance.

# Preface to this version of the memoir

Ten years have elapsed since I finished the first version of this memoir, initially written for my family only, without any thought of publication. When every so often folks who knew about the memoir inquired whether I would let them read it, I made it clear to them that these pages were for family consumption only. Besides, I usually added, why would anyone be interested in reading this material anyway? Since 2007 many events occurred in my life and in the world. Given these personal and global developments, I have often thought that the memoir needed to be brought up to date but, frankly, I just did not find the courage to undertake the task.

Then, in 2015, I received an inquiry from the President of the Wilma Dykeman Legacy, Jim Stokely, who wanted to know whether I would be willing to have the memoir published by the Legacy. Again, my first thought was, "Why would anyone want to read this material?" But in a subsequent conversation, Jim Stokely convinced me to the contrary and I acquiesced to his request. Out of these conversations issued a mutual decision to shorten the volume and to redesign it for public readership. Reducing over 400 pages to roughly 150 pages is not an easy task in terms of selection of relevant texts and editing. Without the editing help generously offered by my daughter Elizabeth Ziffer of Gainesville, Florida, and the support of my second daughter Deborah Ziffer Goodman of New York City, I would not have undertaken the job.

Needless to say, I am grateful to Jim and Anne Stokely of the Wilma Dykeman Legacy for their interest in my life and work. I appreciate Jim Stokely's and Elaine Smyth's careful copy-editing of the text and the valuable suggestions made by the Publishing Committee of the Wilma Dykeman Legacy.

May the following pages be both of interest and usefulness to the reader.

~ Weaverville, 2016

# PART ONE
## *My Early Years*

## CHAPTER 1
# My first prayer

*"Lieber Gott*
*mach mich fromm*
*dass ich in den Himmel komm." (German prayer)*

"Dear God,
Make me pious
That I may go to heaven."

My mother Anny, *z"l* (may her memory be a blessing), bends over me in the baby crib and encourages me to repeat this little German rhymed prayer after her. I look alternately at her and at the little picture at the footboard of the crib. Mutti, as my sister Edith and I called her, notices my wandering eyes between her and the pictures and very earnestly says to me, "Walti, you like those little angels in heaven, don't you?" I sleepily nod my head in agreement. It is these little putti, with golden hair, stubby little wings and rosy cheeks above and below, that hold my attention before I fall asleep. The picture of the baby angels and my mother's face, so kind and loving, blend into one another and I blissfully doze off.

Mutti was a firm believer in God. My father, whom we called Tati, *z"l* (may his memory be a blessing), was an agnostic. Mutti lit candles Friday night to inaugurate the Shabbat or Sabbath, the strict requirements of which none of us followed. As far back as I remember, there was none in our extended family either who observed the Sabbath legislation or any of the other Jewish religious laws. The only religious requirement my parents did observe was fasting on Yom Kippur, the Day of Atonement. I remember that fact quite well because of the less than pleasant mouth odor emanating both from my parents as they embraced and kissed me, as well as from other worshipers at the synagogue who, saying kind words to me, brought their mouths too close to my nose on some of these occasions.

The difference in religious orientation between my mother and father came to the fore when Mutti lovingly chided Tati with, "Leo, you better be careful with your words, especially in front of the children! Some day you will have to justify your less-than-devout stance before the 'lieber Gott.'" The "dear God" was the name by which everyone in our family referred to the Almighty.

What I have been telling here happened long before the war. In those days no Jew spent a whole lot of time cogitating about the reality of God, let alone God's attributes or behavior. If anyone did, I sure don't remember having heard any such discussions. But then I realize that I was only a child at the time. God-talk in our family did not begin until the late 1930s, after Adolf Hitler had firmly established himself as *Führer* of Germany and had become a menace to the rest of the world.

As I reminisce about those early years of my childhood and more particularly about that prayer that Mutti so lovingly and innocently taught me, a prayer that has remained with me to this day and constitutes more than a mere pleasant memory, I cannot help but wonder about the meaning of the words.

"Dear": Refers to someone regarded with deep affection. Having experienced God's absence or silence during the Holocaust, is it honest or even possible at all to address the deity with the adjective "dear"?

"God": To whom or to what are we addressing our prayer? Do we know anything about the recipient of these words? There is in the siddur, the Jewish prayer book, a text called "Hymn of Glory." Its author is Rabbi Judah (died 1217) of Regensburg, Germany who, as we can surmise from the date, lived during the Crusades that wrought deadly havoc on Jewry. In this hymn, sung in many synagogues just prior to the removal of the holy Torah scrolls from the ark that houses them, we hear the words:

> "Melodies I weave, songs I sweetly sing;
> longing for Your Presence, to You I yearn to cling…
> *Without having seen You* I declare Your praise;
> *without having known You* I laud You and Your ways…
> *They have imagined You, but never as You are,*
> they tell of Your deeds, to portray You from afar…
> May You find sweet and pleasing my prayer and my song;
> my soul goes out in yearning, for You alone it longs."
> 
> *(Italics mine)*

Rabbi Judah of Regensburg was an honest man. Already then, long ago, he realized that God could only be imagined and if imagined, it could be done only as one with human-like features. Thus the question that arises immediately is, did this God create humans or did humans create this God?

"Make me pious": In my relationship with God am I a marionette-like being? If it were up to God alone and if the piety of humans were his desire, would God not make every human being pious? To what extent is it *my* obligation and *my* responsibility to be a pious person? Where does human free-will enter the picture? Is there any merit in piety when it is bestowed on me whether I like it or not? I realize, of course, that these are basic conundrums which philosophers and theologians have bandied around *ad infinitum* for many centuries.

"That I may go to heaven": How do I "go" to heaven? What locomotion am I to use? Does this refer to this life or the next, after my death, if, indeed, there is such a thing as heaven? And where and what is the locality referred to as heaven? A real, geographically determined place, or a metaphor? And what happens there, if anything?

While the prayer Mutti taught me is not a typical Jewish prayer but rather more characteristic of assimilated German-speaking Jewry in Europe, it evokes questions similar to the ones Rabbi Judah of Regensburg intimates in his *shir ha-kavod* or Hymn of Glory. Living in tumultuous and for the Jews often deadly times and being keenly aware of God's eerie silence, the Rabbi honestly voiced the inexorable fact that in the final analysis we Jews who lay claim to a whole library dealing with God called the Bible, have not seen or known this God. How did Rabbi Judah's statements that come close to heresy enter the prayer book? Because, in the end, the good Rabbi, despite his honestly admitted lack of clear knowledge about God, glorifies him.

While living at the time of the Crusades, the Inquisition, the Black Death, that decimated the European population, the Blood Libels and the various resulting pogroms that shook Jewish life to its foundation, must have been terrible, the twentieth century Holocaust significantly trumped those events by its bureaucratic absolute brutality and inescapability. Conversion to Christianity in the Middle Ages, whether forced or voluntary, while tragic enough, mitigated the ultimate danger of being murdered. In most cases, death was then still avoidable. This was no longer the case during the Holocaust. Alleged fatal flaws in the racial makeup of which the Jews were accused could not be erased by conversion to Christianity. Only the extermination of the flawed race that endangered the rest of humanity was now considered the sole and ultimate remedy. Thus the Holocaust with its six million Jewish victims and its aftereffects on thousands more even after its cessation.

## My first prayer

Our nuclear family survived this supreme calamity. Fourteen of our closest relatives were murdered. Life after this tragedy never was the same again.

When today I ponder the immediate postwar years, I regret not having discussed with my parents God and God's seeming absence from the theater of unspeakable horror that concentration camp life and death brought about.

Before the outbreak of World War II, I remember Mutti lighting candles in a pair of tall beautiful silver candelabras. Placing them on top of the treadle Singer sewing machine on a crocheted doily, she observed the age-old Jewish ritual of ushering in the Sabbath on Friday evening or as it is called in Yiddish, "*bentshing* light." Edith and I always watched with wide open eyes as Mutti piously muttered the blessing and then, with a thrice repeated graceful circular movement of her hands, encompassing the flames, brought their light to her closed eyes. I do not remember Mutti lighting Sabbath candles after the war. Tati, after the war, had become very silent. Most of the time he just sat there listening to the radio. My own life had taken a definitive turn which resulted in non-communication between my parents and myself. The close and happy life we all experienced before the war had come to an end. The two years I spent with my parents and my sister after the war before my emigration to the United States via France were oriented toward acquiring the trade of auto mechanics. From this apprenticeship I daily returned home filthy and dog tired. God was definitely not on my agenda at age eighteen as a Holocaust survivor.

Also, at this point there was nothing like a Jewish community in our town. The near to one thousand Jews deported by the Nazis in June of 1942 had all been murdered at Auschwitz. Tati had resumed the presidency of the Jewish community of the city of Český Těšín, Czechoslovakia, but there was no one to preside over.

What followed for me was a new life. Whether it represents my search for God or not, I cannot honestly say. If there was such thing as a search for the deity, it certainly was not conscious on my part. But then again, are we human beings always aware of whether we act consciously or unconsciously?

CHAPTER 2
# My first tastes of antisemitism

When Holocaust survivors speak about their experiences, they often begin with something like this: "Life was good for us in Germany (or some other country). Then, one day, we woke up in the morning and everything had changed. Overnight we had become outlaws." The "overnight" refers for German Jews to Hitler's ascendancy to power in 1933 and the subsequent orgies of brutality perpetrated by his *Sturmabteilung* (SA), *Schutzstaffel* (SS) and various other Nazi paramilitary and military units against the German Jewish population or, for Jews living in other Central European countries, to the Nazi invasion of their respective lands and the overtly cruel antisemitic consequences that followed soon after.

This kind of introduction to the Holocaust events is a more sentimental than objective description of the state of affairs that prevailed in most central European countries before the advent of Hitler, leaving us with the impression that for the Jews all was just peachy then. The truth of the matter is that it wasn't quite that way, alas.

Beginning as early as in the early second century C.E., antisemitism had firmly established itself in Christian circles not only in Europe but also in Asia Minor and certain areas of Africa. The blame for the underlying hate philosophy and for the resulting violent acts directed against Jewish populations must be placed on a number of New Testament texts that suggest that it was the Jews who were not only responsible for Jesus' death by collaborating with Rome, but that it was the Jews who actually crucified him, as the late Gospel of John would have us believe (19:16-20). Secondly, there was also much hateful anti-Jewish propaganda emanating from a group of the so-called church fathers, in the form of sermons and tractates that have been preserved to this day.

While much of this venomous literature can be found in the works of a number of these very influential church leaders, bishops, presbyters and theologians, let me cite at this point two examples that should more than adequately suffice to demonstrate the viciousness openly expressed in the literary genre called the *adversos Judaeos* tradition that demonizes the Jews. The examples that follow were penned by Justin Martyr (2nd century C.E.) and John Chrysostom (4th century C.E.), respectively. Justin Martyr writes:

> *For the circumcision according to the flesh, which is from Abraham, was given for a sign, that you [Jews] may be separated from other nations and from us, and that you alone may suffer that which you now suffer, and that your land may be desolate and your cities burned with fire, and that strangers may eat your fruit in your presence and not one of you may go up to Jerusalem.*

With regard to Jewish circumcision, mentioned in the above quote from the second century C.E., I well remember the times when Jewish boys in my home country Czechoslovakia were accosted by gentile boys, forced to drop their pants to have their penis publicly exposed, and be viciously mocked because of their circumcision. The psychological damage done to little boys accosted in this manner can be easily imagined. Fear and even dread of having this shameful violation forced upon them haunted them every time they went to relieve themselves in the schools' restrooms. One can only guess to what extent their self-esteem and their very psyche were damaged because of what was tantamount to rape. Group showering in army facilities was a dreaded moment for Jewish soldiers because under these circumstances their circumcision was visible to their fellows and became an opportunity for antisemitic derisory remarks and embarrassment to the Jewish young men.

The church father Chrysostom of Antioch, whose name means "golden-mouthed," an epithet earned by his powerful preaching, went even further than Justin:

> *When animals have been fattened by having all they want to eat, they get stubborn and hard to manage…. When animals are unfit for work, they are marked for slaughter, and this is the very thing which the Jews have experienced. By making themselves unfit for work, they have become ready for slaughter.*

It is evident from these and many similar sermonic statements from the "golden mouth" of *Saint* Chrysostom, a poison-spewing church father after whom a whole liturgy was eventually named, that God and all godly men, prophets and martyrs, passionately hate the Jews. While Chrysostom apparently does not go so far as to overtly advise his listeners to perpetrate violence against the Jews, one cannot help but wonder whether his words about "slaughter" are meant merely metaphorically or physically. History has shown that ambiguous statements such as these, uttered by prestigious personalities, were often understood according to their plain meaning. Christians, on countless occasions, incited by similar incendiary rhetoric took it upon themselves to inflict injury and even death on these allegedly abominable Jews who had crucified their own messiah, the Lord Jesus Christ.

Relatively few Christians ever heard the name of either one of these church leaders. Some would argue that whatever may have been said centuries ago, had it been ever so hateful, would have had at the very most merely a local impact. Not so! Church gatherings and sermons of famous preachers, long into the Middle Ages and beyond, had an enormously powerful impact on the gathered public. Church attendance was often an all-day affair. The church was nothing less than the very center of people's social life. Religion then was not as marginal an occupation in people's lives as it often is today. The truth of the matter is that antisemitism bored itself deeply into the Christian populations' ethos and, fortified over succeeding centuries by men equally gifted in the art of religious hatemongering like Justin, Chrysostom and others, produced a lingering poisonous residue that has, in too many cases, continued festering on in peoples' minds to this day. This antisemitic toxicity survived into the twentieth century and was in evidence in our small town of Český Těšín even in my own time.

One of the two best friends I had in our town was Jakob Katz. We were of the same age and attended the same class in the elementary *Masaryková Škola*, the elementary school named after Czechoslovakia's first president Tomáš Garrigue Masaryk. Jakob was the son of a Jewish tailor who lived in a very small modest house, some five blocks from the apartment house on the main street, named *Saská Kupa* (in German Sachsenberg), where we occupied the whole second floor. My father was a well-respected attorney in town, and it seemed to my four-years-older sister Edith and to me that everybody knew him. No wonder! On our Sunday morning walks practically every person we encountered lifted his hat respectfully before my father with the greeting, "*Guten Morgen, Herr Doktor!*" In response to our question, "Tati, who was that?" his standard answer was, "If God does not know him better than I, he is in deep trouble."

It was my father who represented the Jewry of our town and county vis-à-vis the local government. He also was the president of the synagogue and so, in all probability, most of our town's people,

*My first tastes of antisemitism*

not to mention the Jewish population, really knew who he was. We were a middle class or, at best, an upper middle class family, and one could say that we were strongly assimilated Jews, as I already indicated. The Katz family, on the other hand, occupied the lower rungs of our town's societal ladder. As Orthodox Jews they practiced their faith assiduously. On the social level the Ziffer and the Katz families had nothing in common except their Jewishness. In retrospect I cannot help but express shame that our Jewish population was so heavily socially stratified. It is a fact and nothing to be proud of that we, assimilationists that we were, actually looked down on the Orthodox elements among us. To a certain extent there was even embarrassment that these Orthodox Jews, the *Hasidim* ("pious Jews") or "Polish Jews" (German: *polnische Juden*), as we called them, had a life style significantly different from, and in our opinion, inferior to ours. They had their own little one-room synagogues called *shtiblakh* (Yiddish: plural from *shtibl* meaning little room); they dressed differently from us; they wore long earlocks (Yiddish: *peyes*) tightly wound into descending spirals, hanging down in front of their ears often as low as their shoulders as well as, in the case of their adult men, long beards. They wore long black kaftans that were not always clean and strange head covers. The boys wore little stiff cylindrical black caps with a small visor while the men wore either black broad-brimmed hats or head coverings consisting of a black cloth round center piece sitting on the crown of their heads attached to a surrounding rim of sable or fox fur, a *shtreimel* as it is called in Yiddish. All the married women had their hair cropped and wore wigs covered by scarves. The Polish Jews spoke Yiddish and to our embarrassment rarely spoke our national Czech language correctly. Emanating from the *shtiblakh*, especially on Friday evenings, were shouting, singing, the sound of wild dancing and at times woeful moaning, all in Ashkenaz Hebrew and Yiddish. Passers-by often stopped when hearing this cacophony and, with their noses glued against the windows, tried to make out what the hubbub inside was all about. More often than not they would then mockingly smile and with telling gestures, such as fingers tapping at their temples, suggest something like "too bad we have to put up with these crazies." To be honest and to my regret I must say that many of us assimilated Jews identified with these *goyishe* (Yiddish for non-Jewish) folks' sentiments. Proud we definitely were not of the Polish Jews among us, and this is an understatement.

None of this bothered me with regard to Jakob who was the son of Polish Jews. Sure, he too looked a bit strange compared to the other boys I knew, but we were friends and that's what counted. Besides, as I heard Mutti say on a good many occasions, "Your friend Jakob is such a beautiful little boy. He doesn't look like one of them. Just look at his olive complexion, his blue eyes and his aquiline nose!" Little Jakob was truly a very handsome boy.

Strange as this may sound, I do not remember ever having seen Jakob in our apartment despite our friendship. Nor did I ever enter the Katz's little single floor home. Could it be that our families' different Jewish religious alignment prohibited such contact?

One day we walked home together, Jakob and I. Our return trip took us at one point to a dark underpass of the railroad that passed overhead. As we walked down there, with our satchels on our backs, we suddenly heard shouts of "*žid, špinavý židek*" (Jew, filthy little Jew) and rocks starting flying at us. Shielding our faces from these projectiles with our hands as best we could, we started running for our lives, Jakob to the right and I to the left. Out of breath, I reached the entrance to a nearby apartment house and there took shelter. Carefully peeking through the glass entrance door, I realized that there was no one pursuing me. But my heart sank at what I saw happening outside. A small horde of boys was close to catching little Jakob. In a flash of mind it came to me that once caught they would pull down his pants and…

But at this very moment there galloped onto the scene our town idiot, *Der Blöde* (The Stupid One), as everyone called him. This was a tall man with a weather-worn deeply wrinkled face and blond wavy hair falling down to his shoulders. It was he who, pulling a two-wheeled cart, picked up the droppings from the horses and other trash in the gutters. It was he also who, parading through town and holding high a large placard, announced the coming to town of the circus, an annual affair anticipated by all with much joy. There were mischievous boys in our town who would run after him, call him names, mockingly berate him. On such occasions he'd suddenly turn around, face them and roar at them. To me who saw this happen many times, his roar, with mouth wide open and his yellow large rotten teeth protruding, truly resembled the roar of a lion. Whenever this happened the cruel but now frightened boys stopped in their tracks and rapidly fell back.

On this occasion *Der Blöde* appeared suddenly as if out of nowhere. With a mighty swoop of his arms he picked up little Jakob and placed him on his two-wheeled cart and galloped away. I was reminded of the charioteers in *Ben Hur*, one of my favorite books: my friend Jakob – a Jewish charioteer! It was wondrous how my little friend was rescued.

When the boys dispersed I came out of the hiding place and rapidly walked home. Mutti, having heard my story, took me into her arms and, stroking my hair, reassured me with, "Walti, forget this incident! These boys are nothing but ignorant *Lausbuben* (street urchins)."

I have never been able to forget this incident!

Why this Jew-hatred? Where and how might these "street urchins" have acquired the Jew-hating attitude? The only logical and historically documented response is, of course, from their priests and preachers directly or via their parents and other relatives. And why? Because for centuries the churches had been erroneously but intentionally teaching that it was the Jews who killed Jesus Christ, God the Son. Although never experienced personally, I know from Jewish friends here in America that they, on occasion, had been called Christ-killers.

Justin Martyr, Saint Chrysostom *et al.* had done a thorough job disseminating Jew hatred many centuries before Hitler's arrival on the world scene. "What is sown is reaped."

Was I aware of antisemitism as a little boy? It was impossible not to be!

My father told us the following story that deeply impressed both Edith and me. It happened on April 1, 1899, in Polná, a small town on the border between Bohemia and Moravia, just before Passover and Easter whose dates often coincide. These two geographical entities constitute today the Czech Republic. In those days, while largely ethnically Czech, the lands were part of the Austro-Hungarian Empire. A young woman, a seamstress, nineteen years old, not having returned home nor having shown up at the shop for three days, was eventually found dead in a nearby forest, nude with her throat slit. The town was understandably in an uproar over the crime. Shortly after finding her, one of the bystanders cried out, "Look here people: the girl was *kosher* butchered!" (kosher meaning according to Jewish ritual animal slaughter law). No sooner said, and the mob stormed to the Jewish quarter of Polná, raising havoc, smashing windows and looting Jewish establishments and homes. To this mob it was immediately clear that the murder had been committed by the Jews who needed Christian blood for the manufacture of the *matzos*, the unleavened bread that Jewish law mandates be eaten during Passover. The victim was quickly found: a certain Leopold Hilsner, a homeless Jewish vagabond, unemployed and a good for nothing. Without delay witnesses were found who allegedly saw him in company of two other drifters forcing the young woman into the woods. The few witnesses who vouched for Hilsner's innocence were intimidated with threats against their lives. The local clergy enthusiastically supported the accusing mob, inciting them even further. It came to trial in the city of Kutná Hora, and the attorney who defended Hilsner, a very decent Christian man by the name of Dr. Auředníček, in whose office my father clerked after his law studies in Vienna, fell ill from despair

## My first tastes of antisemitism

about his powerlessness to help innocent Hilsner. It seems that Dr. Baxa who was appointed as replacement for Auředníček as Hilsner's defense attorney, acted even worse than the state prosecutor. Hilsner received the death penalty even though no proof of his guilt was produced. In the end it was Professor Masaryk of Charles University in Prague, later to become Czechoslovakia's first president, who, trying to expose the terrible medieval superstition of "blood libel" for what it was, namely an antisemitic invention that had grown deep roots in the Christian population of Central Europe and beyond, succeeded in procuring statements from a number of European university scholars stating that the Blood Libel accusations against the Jews was pure nonsense. He, too, was threatened for his stance in the Hilsner case but insisted on fighting it out. As a result of the intervention of this prestigious academic, Hilsner was retried in the town of Písek and, for the second time, was sentenced to death. It was the emperor who commuted his sentence to a lifelong prison sentence, and Hilsner spent the next nineteen years in prison. When the empire collapsed he was granted amnesty, and he emigrated to Vienna where his fellow Jews supported him. He died at the age of fifty-nine.

His defense counsel, Dr. Auředníček, because of his activity in favor of Hilsner, lost all his friends and clients so that in the end he, too, emigrated to Vienna. Only with great difficulty was he able to rebuild his professional activity there. To his death he remained the best of friends with Masaryk.

Ironically the identity of the real murderer of the young woman had been known all along to the populace of Polná. He was a vagabond who had been apprehended and imprisoned no less than fourteen times for attempted murder, rape and robbery. This real criminal lived out his life peacefully as a chimney sweep.

This is the story my father told us. It was fully corroborated by the detailed account of the Hilsner affair in the Czech language transcript of the trial which I eventually acquired with the help of my sister. It sits on the shelf of my library and it makes me tremble every time my eyes fall on it. Was I, as a child, aware of antisemitism? The answer is: yes.

In 1937, when I was ten years old, there happened an event in our town that throws further light on the pre-war Polish and Czech antisemitism. An old Polish Hasidic Jew, with a long grey beard, sidelocks under a black hat, and clothed in a black kaftan reaching to his ankles, set out from somewhere in Poland to rejoin members of his family in Czechoslovakia and arrived in Cieszyn, one of the border towns between the two countries. There are three bridges that lead over the Olza River, which defines the border. On each side of the main bridge which the old man wished to cross stood then a small wooden building, a *budka*, housing the border guards. It was at the budkas that one was required to present one's crossing permit. The old Jew did just that on the Polish side and was allowed to proceed. When he arrived on the Czech side, the same procedure was required but here, alas, he ran into a snag. The Czech border police, for reasons that escape me today, did not find his documents in order and refused him entry into Czechoslovakia. They told him to return to Poland. The old Jew, schlepping a shabby suitcase and a bundle holding his other possessions, argued with the Czechs but to no avail. With no choice other than to return to Poland, he turned around and shuffled back to the Polish side of the bridge. There he explained his dilemma to the Poles who, however, refused to understand the old Jew's dilemma. What happened was clearly not their but the Czechs' problem, they countered. Once he had left Poland with his exit visa, they could not allow him to reenter their land. So what now?

So back to the Czech side the old Jew went, not knowing what to do now. One of the Czech gendarmes, taking pity on the old man, called my father in his capacity of president of the Jewish community of Český Těšín. Tati went to the bridge. There the old man implored him to help. After lengthy deliberations with the border gendarmes, he received permission to have a small shack built at the exact middle of the bridge to house the old Jew until the problem would be resolved. The primitive wood shack was erected very quickly and the old Jew subsequently spent several days living in the middle of the bridge while my father spent much time on the phone with the authorities. I was one of the children who brought provisions to the old man during that time. We also emptied his bucket from high up into the river. I thought that was fun. There was no way of conversing with the man because he spoke only some Polish and Yiddish, two languages I could not handle in those days. And even had we been able to engage in conversation, what would we have talked about? The Bible? Talmud or Midrash?

I remember seeing the old man every so often *shockeling*, swaying back and forth in prayer, when I arrived. Despite my young age I realized even then already that the old Jew lived in a world different from mine. For the folks crossing the bridge he presented a veritable spectacle. There was laughing and sneering; for antisemites this was a dream fulfilled. Luckily for him, my father was successful in resolving the impasse by procuring for him the necessary permit to enter Czechoslovakia. It is more than likely that the old man's enjoyment of family and new country did not last long. The probability is high, alas, that he and his family were murdered by the Germans who invaded our republic two years later. The story speaks for itself with regard to pre-war antisemitism.

During the card playing get-togethers that took place regularly on Sunday afternoons at my grandparents' home on the Polish side of our divided town of Teschen, at which my parents and my local uncles and aunts participated in a smoke-filled living room, and from which political talk was hardly ever absent in those days, I once overheard my uncle Emil say the phrase that is well known to Jews everywhere: "*Shver tzi zayn a yid*." (It's hard to be a Jew.) That evening I sat in my sister Edith's brass bed for our usual evening palaver. I asked her did she know the meaning of the phrase. She, four years older than I and ever the wise one, looked at me with an enigmatic smile and said, "Walti, don't worry about it. It's just talk. But if you think you must know, ask Tati." I never asked.

At age ten or eleven I knew that Jews were not liked, even in our town, despite all the respect that was usually shown to my father by non-Jews. My sister and I attended religious instruction given by Herr Müller, a diminutive little man who instructed us in German about Jewish history and taught us to translate Bible verses by rote. What boredom that was! Neither the problem of antisemitism nor any question concerning God and how the latter might relate to this phenomenon, or the phrase of Uncle Emil's that puzzled me, was ever evoked. The time was not ripe for questions of this kind…at least not yet.

## CHAPTER 3
## Polish takeover

My mother was an avid stamp collector, following in the footsteps of her brother Oscar, who was known for having one of the finest stamp collections in Czechoslovakia. She specialized in Czech, Polish, German, Austro-Hungarian and Austrian stamps. Often she sat into the night handling the newly purchased stamps very meticulously with special pincers and placing them into the appropriate albums. I heard my father tease her every so often: "Anny, when did you make acquaintance with Mr. Mendelsohn?" who appeared among other famous music geniuses in a composers series, referring, of course, to the recent purchase she had made.

Enjoying her handling of the stamps, I would often sit with her admiring these little miniatures of famous men, architectural monuments, animals, etc. On one of these occasions, Mutti brought home a large stamp framed in black with the picture of a man on it. "Why the black frame?" I asked. "This is Austrian chancellor Dollfuss," she replied somberly. "He was assassinated by a band of Nazis." The year was 1934.

Dark storm clouds gathered over Europe. Hitler began to be seen as a dangerous menace to European peace. In the Sunday afternoon card games his name was being evoked with ever greater frequency. I was too young to understand. My great uncle Arnold, brother of my grandmother Hermine, was a large man with a powerful voice. It was he who was heard most often. One of the phrases that kept on ringing in my ears was, "*Ich hör' sie schon trappeln*" (I already hear them galloping), a reference to Soviet Russia's cavalry that would soon attack Hitler's army and defeat them. A pipedream if ever there was one.

Austria fell to the Nazis on March 12, 1938.

Shortly afterwards, my father, an enthusiastic Rotarian, was apprised that the Rotary Club of Linz, Austria, had introduced the so-called *Arier Paragraph*, the regulation that non-Aryans were not allowed to join or maintain their membership in Rotary International. When he heard this, he became livid with rage. This meant of course that Jews, defined as non-Aryans by the Nazi Nuremberg Laws passed in 1935, were from here on banned from membership in Rotary clubs. Rushing to his typewriter he banged out a protest letter to the Rotary Club in Linz and a letter to the Rotary International headquarters in Chicago, informing the latter of the illegality of the Austrian club's action under Rotary's international charter.

Tati was, in my opinion, what we call a "Renaissance man," highly educated and of a liberal spirit. With him anyone was able to discuss most any subject. Yet Tati was naive in this and other worldly matters. Perhaps he was too much of an optimist, unable even to imagine the sinister machinations of Hitler and too trusting in our fellow Europeans' sense of justice and willingness to fight for it.

Needless to say, neither Linz nor Chicago bothered to respond to his indignant letters. Tati should have at this point become aware of the ominous situation that was about to develop for us, living as we were in close proximity to both Germany and Austria. Perhaps he was – and simply did not allow himself to admit it.

Then came another wakeup call. Later that year we received the totally unexpected visit of Friedl, a distant cousin of my mother's who lived in Vienna. He arrived very hurriedly with a small suitcase under his arm. After ravenously eating a meal my mother set before him, he closeted himself with Tati and Mutti in our living room. Mutti escorted us to the kitchen and told us to remain there until called. Edith and I knew instinctively that something very important was taking place among them. That evening Friedl disappeared, never to be seen again. In the end my parents felt obligated to share with us what had taken place.

Friedl had come to us as a refugee from Vienna. He told about the hundreds of suicides committed by Viennese Jews after the so-called *Anschluss* – the incorporation of Austria into the greater German Reich. The Viennese Jews saw the handwriting on the wall and despaired of what they knew would follow in terms of Jew persecutions. Tati, it seems, was at first skeptical of Friedl's account. Because the man requested money so that he could continue his flight toward the East, Tati became suspicious concerning the veracity of the horror stories Friedl told. Did the man flee Vienna for reasons other than his fear of Nazi persecution? Did he perhaps commit a crime? When Tati voiced these doubts, albeit in a sensitive manner, Friedl removed his shirt and displayed his chest and back. They were covered with circular scars. By extinguishing cigarettes on Friedl's body, the SS tortured him to spill the names of Jews who allegedly belonged to an anti-Nazi resistance ring of which Friedl himself was allegedly a member. Seeing the scars sufficed to convince my father. Friedl got the money he requested, and after being served a second hearty meal by my ever-compassionate mother, disappeared into the dark.

The event shook us up.

1938 was a very bad year for us. Our town lay in northern Moravia, in an area called Silesia on the border with Poland. Its name was Český Těšín, meaning Czech Teschen, in contradistinction to Polish Teschen or Cieszyn, the name of the town on the other side of the Olza River. It was the river that divided the former single city which carried the German name Teschen prior to 1918, when

Czechoslovakia and Poland were formed from part of the collapsed Austro-Hungarian Empire.

During the critical time of the Munich Conference in September 1938, Hitler secured the much coveted Sudeten portion of Czechoslovakia. In trying to appease Hitler's expansionary appetite, Great Britain, France and the Soviet Union had abandoned the one truly democratic outpost in Central Europe that Czechoslovakia represented. During this crisis the Polish government renewed its longstanding claims to the Teschen region. The Poles submitted an ultimatum to the Czechs on September 29, exploiting the moment of Czechoslovakia's agony at its loss of the Sudeten region, and on October 2, 1938, the Czech government yielded to Polish demands. That very day Polish forces occupied our town and its vicinity, some 400 square miles with some 240,000 inhabitants. The area was rich in coal mines and boasted the second largest Czech steel production facility in nearby Třinec, the birthplace of my mother.

Overnight we had become Poles.

I still remember clearly the Polish military occupation of our town and especially its pompous Jewish corollary: the Polish Rabbi Eisenstein and the cantor, dressed in their ceremonial robes and hats, accompanied by some Polish Jewish synagogue officials, strutting across the Olza bridge and extending their religious hegemony over us defeated Czech fellow Jews, and appropriating our synagogues. It was a demoralizing and even disgusting sight for Edith and me, the children of Tati, the president of the Czech Jewish community and synagogues, now demoted from his post. All this boded ill for the future.

And not only did our father lose his status as president of our area's Jewry. He also lost his livelihood, not being licensed to practice law in Poland. In view of my mother's selling off our Persian carpets one by one, certain pieces of china, silver flatware, jewelry – objects she valued very highly from a monetary as well as sentimental viewpoint – we must not have had significant savings to fall back on. The other

## Polish takeover

members of our family living on the formerly Czech side of town fared much better than my father. Not being professionals who needed to be licensed to carry on their occupation, they essentially continued in their old jobs. To my mother and father it was scandalous that none of these relatives came to our aid during this dire time.

After many of these heart-wrenching selloffs, my mother took a course making pastries and candles. She peddled these homemade products to weddings, bar mitzvahs and similar Jewish celebratory events, making just enough money to keep our heads above water. For my father, the time was disgraceful and depressing, especially vis-à-vis the rest of the family whose lifestyle was in no way affected.

It was during the following summer that mother's sister Steffie, living in the Polish city of Katowice, invited me to spend a couple of weeks with them. Her husband Jacqui was chief chemist in a large industrial corporation, a highly respected professional who had earned fifty or so patents in the field.

A few memories stand out for me from that last pre-war vacation with them. They owned a Škoda convertible sedan and I loved sitting next to my uncle, watching every move he made while driving. I learned to ride a bicycle in the inner court of their apartment house. That was a lot of fun. In the process I became friends with my little cousin George, two years my junior. George was a whiz in geography and struck me as a veritable walking encyclopedia in that field. George also played the accordion, and that impressed me. Finally, Aunt Steffie usually served us cold fruit soups at noon, something my mother had never done before. I especially enjoyed her cherry soup.

When I returned home to my parents, Aunt Steffie invited my sister Edith to join them on a little vacation in the Polish Tatra Mountains, at the famous resort of Zakopane. Steffie and Jacqui were the only relatives who noticed my family's dire needs and came to our assistance. My mother would never forget it. In this connection she often quoted the English proverb my father had taught her: "Friends in need are friends indeed." The only other two English proverbs she enjoyed quoting were, "A hungry man is an angry man," and "Roses are red, violets are blue, honey is sweet and so are you." Oh, what a delightful woman she was!

With the Polish occupation upon us, my sister and I were forced to attend Polish school. Wearing student uniforms was obligatory: navy suit and overcoat with gold buttons, and a blue cap with a shiny black visor. I hated the costume. In sixth grade or, according to the Polish system, the first grade of lyceum, some teachers taunted us both as defeated Czechs and, more importantly, as Jews. One of my teachers would pretend to speak to me in Yiddish in front of the whole class, which left my fellow students in stitches and me, of course, deeply embarrassed. Furthermore, those obligatory religion classes under that pompous ass Rabbi Eisenstein, clad in his black clerical robe on these occasions, left both my sister and me in virtual despair. We hated the man but had no choice in the matter.

We both prayed, and this is no exaggeration, that something might happen to end this miserable situation. We sadly recalled the good times when my father and mother had been cheerful and when our family life had been joyful, full of fun adventures. Now it had become pure drudgery and depressing.

One evening our parents announced that they would spend the night at the grandparents' house, across the river. The next morning they returned and broke the sad news that Omama, as we called our grandmother, had died that night. After a stroke she had become bound to a wheelchair. Her talk had become slurred so that we could not understand her, but her eyes continued radiating love for Edith and me. I don't remember having participated at the funeral.

When much later in the 1980's, during my five-year stay in Nova Scotia, a clergyman retiring from his position in Liverpool told me that he would be volunteering as an English teacher in the town of Cieszyn in Poland, the very town in which my grandparents had lived,

## Polish takeover

I asked him to visit the Jewish cemetery there and try finding the gravesite of my grandparents, Jakob and Hermine Borger. He kindly did just that, but was unable to find the graves because the cemetery had become a veritable jungle. Photographs he brought back showed tombstones literally enveloped by tree trunks that had grown around them with grass and weeds three feet high, just about everywhere.

The Hebrew term for cemetery is *gan chayyim* or "garden of life." Knowing that tombstones are erected in order to keep alive the remembrance of the departed, the photographs from the Teschen cemetery made me very sad. Then I began wondering whether the trees' embrace of these memorial stones perhaps suggested that nature itself claimed the dead into its own ever ongoing cycle of life. For is not the loving embrace of those cold and inanimate stones by living nature precisely the fulfillment of the words we say at Jewish funerals: "May his/her soul be bound up in the bond of life!" After all, nothing is a more meaningful symbol of life than a tree, representative par excellence of that nature of which we all are an integral part, whether living or dead. The thought has been a solace to me.

My much admired teacher Barukh (or Benedict) Spinoza (1632-1677) is famous for having written *deus sive natura*, meaning "God or nature." By being embraced by nature, those cold stones and whom they represent may just be embraced by God. Reminds me of the end of Deuteronomy, when according to the Midrash God takes Moses' life with a kiss.

1938 was indeed a difficult year.

## Locations of Nazi camps mentioned in this memoir

PART TWO
*In the Clutches of Evil*

## CHAPTER 4
## Here come the Nazis

Gone were the sunny days of the pre-1938 period. A few snapshots from "Paradise Lost" will have to suffice. Gone were the evenings we listened to opera music with Tati telling us about the composer and the plot, and alerting us to this or that musical theme that characterized a certain aspect of the plot, a theme that would wind itself like a silver thread throughout the composition. Mutti often sang along with the heroine, and Tati would turn to her smilingly, saying, "Do let *her* sing, Anny, OK?" We fell in love with Puccini and Verdi, Mozart and, of course, Beethoven.

Gone were the evenings when with infinite patience my father taught me the game of chess. Once having mastered the fundamentals, we played against each other and often replayed masters' games in order to familiarize ourselves with the various gambits. Names like Alekhine, Euwe, Capablanca, Lasker, Flohr and others became household names.

Gone were the evenings spent with Tati in our improvised dark room, the small bathroom transformed into a shop for developing and enlarging photographs he had taken. Tati owned two fine cameras: a Zeiss Ikon and a Rolleiflex. In the pitch dark with only a small red light glowing, I remember him leaning over shallow glass containers which he rocked back and forth to cover the photographic paper immersed there in mixtures of various chemical liquids. Slowly, ever so slowly – downright magically – there emerged on the wet papers, images. These grew stronger and stronger until fully developed. After fixing the images in another glass bowl, he rinsed them under the faucet and then hung them by wooden clips on strings strung on the other side of the bathroom. There they dried, in preparation for further processing. Then, one unforgettable day, I was allowed to do all this work myself under his supervision. An exhilarating experience.

In the *Herrenzimmer*, the parlor, a glass-enclosed library covered one whole wall, with books two deep on each shelf. I knew pretty well the location of each one of the two thousand volumes in the library. Sitting on a small ladder, I would roam through the volumes, looking at the titles and most of all at the pictures. A four-volume beautifully illustrated edition of the Bible sat next to a blue leather-bound edition of the Arabian Nights, also lavishly illustrated. To this day I see before me Scheherezade with one voluptuous breast spilling from her tight fitting robe, lounging on a divan. This was also where Edith discovered a book entitled *The Sexual Life of Woman*. One day I surprised her as she sat on that same small ladder devouring the text and the illustrations of that work. "Don't dare tell Tati or Mutti about this," she warned me, deeply blushing. This was all that I, rascal that I was, needed to hear. From here on I had her in my power, and I used virtually every trick in the book to extort things from her. "Edith, give me so and so…" or "Edith, do such and such…if you don't, I'll tell Mutti that you…" Sometimes I simply used the telltale word "ladder" to make her acquiesce to my wishes. When my mother finally found out the truth behind what was going on, she reassured Edith, "There was nothing wrong in your reading the book, Edith. You need not be ashamed!" With this motherly reassurance, my power over Edith evaporated. Too bad for me! But all this was just a game anyway, a kidding around, sibling fun. Edith and I loved each other dearly.

*Here come the Nazis*

In connection with this library, I have often thought how wisely my father always chose just the right books for Edith and me to read. Frequently we discussed their content with Tati, who on such occasions pointed out to us some of their salient points we had overlooked in our reading. In the earlier years of our childhood, Tati had Edith and me sit at the foot of his bed under the same blanket while he read to us in the evening. And what a reader he was! Reality vividly jumped out at us as he changed his voice, moving from one personage in the plot to the other. I remember how, in the story of Aladdin, Edith and I literally trembled for fear when the genie of the lamp appeared and shouted, "I am the genie of the lamp. What do you desire?" Dickens' *Christmas Carol* in prose was read to us in German as Tati, on this occasion, translated the English text simultaneously for us into German. My father was a premier educator. If I became a good teacher myself – a compliment given to me fairly often – it is he who made this possible by means of his extraordinary pedagogical skills.

Under the library shelves in the *Herrenzimmer* there were cabinets that held some of my mother's table linens, a few games, the wonderful construction sets that were my uncle Ernst's regular birthday gifts, and dozens of bottles of liquor ranging from wine to slivovitz (fruit brandy). This was Mr. Faisal's means of payment of the attorney fees to my father who represented him in a lawsuit. In the process of looking for a game board down there one day, Edith and I discovered the great array of bottles and, among them, Malaga wine. So, why not open this pretty bottle and taste its contents? And so we did. We liked what we drank, and over a period of time Edith and I managed to empty one of those bottles. When my mother found the emptied bottle, all hell broke loose. After a brief interrogation our sin was revealed. Not only did we get our faces slapped, something we did not mind because the slaps were only symbolic and did not hurt a bit, but to our chagrin, that cabinet was locked from then on. The event itself was never forgotten. When as a full grown man, decades later,

I sometimes expressed my disappointment about having remained short at five feet five inches tall, my mother would remind me very earnestly of our shameful youthful transgression with, "*Das musst du halt dem Malaga verdanken!*" (For that you'll have to thank the bottle of Malaga!), which would send all of us into roaring laughter.

The Polish occupation did not last long. Ever darker clouds gathered over Europe and even my uncles and aunts during their Sunday afternoon card games sounded less and less optimistic. The Soviet cavalry refused to show up as my great-uncle Arnold had predicted, and the Jewish population of our town seemed to decrease from day to day. Eventually many of our relatives took off for locations farther east, thinking that in closer proximity to the Soviet Union they would be safe from Hitler's thirst for ever more territory, which none of his additional territorial acquisitions seemed to quench.

Come the morning of September 1, 1939, and we lived in a virtual ghost town. The streets were deserted and an eerie silence had settled in. A lonely plane kept circling in the blue sky above our heads, and I could not shake the feeling that something dramatic was about to take place. Something big was in the making. Our expectations were well-founded. There was this thick, silent but palpable electricity in the air, tension, a feeling of heaviness that precedes the impending storm's first lightning discharge.

My father seemed oblivious to all this. "Walti," he said to me very calmly, "please run over to Uncle Emil and ask him to give you the *Goethe* by Emil Ludwig which he borrowed from me. Its return is long overdue." So I set out to Uncle Emil's apartment, about five blocks away from us. A taxi with running engine stood at the entrance to the building and my uncle, aunt Hermine, and cousins Otto and Lydia were all feverishly running up and down the staircase loading the car with the family's most valuable possessions. When I conveyed Tati's message to my nervous-looking uncle, he shook his head in disbelief and bellowed out a short laugh then ran up and handed the large book

## Here come the Nazis

to me. "Say to your dad that we wish you all good luck. We are going off to Lemberg" (Polish: Lwów). He gave me a pat on the head and ran up the stairs. I thanked Uncle Emil and walked back home. Not a single soul could be seen anywhere – just empty streets and sidewalks. Handing the book into father's hands, I heard him say, "Well, it took him a long time! Thanks, Walti." Calmly Tati walked back to the *Bibliothek*, as we called the large glass-enclosed library, and placed the book into the empty slot that had been waiting to be filled again. I went back to my lookout post at the window next to Edith.

And then a never-before-heard sound came to our ears. Every so often that tumultuous noise was pierced by shrill sharp voices. It came nearer and nearer and then suddenly it was upon us, right under our windows.

The rush of a mass of people, military equipment, domestic animals, horse-mounted soldiers, marching soldiers, peasants on their horse-drawn wagons, goats and sheep – a motley crowd, inundating and streaming through our main street in the direction of the main bridge across the Olza River, eastward. The sound this inchoate avalanche-like flow of human and animal mix made was pierced by commands shouted by officers desperately trying to reestablish some kind of minimum order. What we witnessed below us was a chaotically retreating Polish army and populace before the German forces' relentless onslaught. It was seemingly impossible to slow, let alone stop, the German *Wehrmacht's* (armed forces) advance. The concrete bunkers that had been built by the Czechs precisely for this kind of eventuality, taken over about one year later by the Poles, had not been used at all. Both the Czech and Polish spokespersons for their respective governments had used bombastic words about their will and capability to resist and even to defeat Hitler, but words clearly had not sufficed. Those Polish officers with their colorful turkey feathers on their military hats had always struck us more as operatic figures than as able and determined fighters. It took Hitler only a couple of weeks to defeat the

Polish army. Polish cavalry was no match for German tanks.

It probably took about two hours or so for that chaotic flight to rush by our windows. Then followed silence. I see my father sitting by the radio with a tense expression on his face, trying to make sense out of the excited multi-language garble emanating from the speaker. "Children," he would say to us every so often, "do you see anything new down in the street?"

After a long ominous silence, a new ever-increasing noise came to our ears. This time we were able to recognize it as the sound of engines. As the crescendo peaked, we discovered its sources appearing around the corner and entering Main Street. This time it was trucks pulling artillery pieces, personnel carriers with gray-helmeted German soldiers sitting on rows of benches, tanks, motorcycles with and without sidecars, all in perfect formation. There was not the slightest disorder in this parade-like drive-by. The line of motorized vehicles took the same direction as had the disarrayed fleeing Polish army a bit earlier, across the Olza bridge and toward the east. When the last vehicle passed, there settled upon us once again an oppressive silence – but this time not for long.

To this day I have been wondering how it all happened so quickly and almost imperceptibly. Nazi swastika flags now suddenly hung from a number of houses in our immediate vicinity. Where did these German flags come from? Did our Czech neighbors hang them from their windows? Was all this pre-planned and carefully orchestrated? Out of nowhere men, women and children appeared, now lining the street below, waving small Nazi flags as if awaiting a parade.

And we did not have to wait very long for what was more sinister than a parade. Soon units of black-uniformed SS men (*Schutzstaffel*, commanded by Heinrich Himmler), marching in perfect formation, came into view. There must have been several hundreds of them as they made their entrance to the rousing shouts of welcome by the flag-waving population of our town. *Heil Hitler*, the German salute,

*Here come the Nazis*

was enthusiastically shouted by hundreds of welcoming people down below who had come out of the woodwork to welcome the Nazi occupation troops. We were stunned. Who were these shouting men and women? Were they Czechs or Poles? Traitors? Were they local people or imported rabble-rousers?

The *Heil Hitlers* continued reverberating from below for quite a while as the SS units marched toward the town square. Eventually we lost sight of the black-uniformed marchers and with them the sound of the hated Nazi slogan.

*"Ach Du lieber Gott! Leo, was wird jetzt mit uns geschehen?"* I heard my mother moan. "Oh, dear God, what will happen to us now, Leo?"

We were rid of the hated Polish occupiers, only for them to be replaced by the dreaded Germans.

And there was no sign of the *lieber Gott* anywhere in sight.

CHAPTER 5
# My first love and tragedy

On September 1, 1939, threats to life and liberty in a police state became our daily companions. With the arrival of the *SS* units, we were deprived of our freedom in an instant. We Jews became overnight the official enemies of the Reich and exposed to any whimsy on the part of the Nazis who were the masters of this evil Reich. A bitter foretaste of these death-dealing whimsies – some ordered from up high in the German hierarchy, some invented and executed by local officials or by the ever-present antisemitic mob – was given to us that first night under German occupation.

The day had been hard. All four of us were mentally exhausted and went to bed early. Perhaps we simply wished to forget what had transpired earlier that day. Perhaps we thought that sleep would bring a welcome relief from all that tension we experienced. Contrary to my usual sleeping habits, I woke up early the next morning, around five. I felt nervous, even scared. Conscious of my mental agitation, there was only one thing to do: crawl in bed with Mutti and Tati who would not mind. Searching for my father, I found him standing on the balcony that gave onto the courtyard. Leaning against the metal railing, he stood there straining to identify the strange noises that could be heard. His face, usually ruddy, was very pale now, and it was obvious that he was deeply troubled. Happy to have found my beloved Tati, I ran up to him. "Why aren't you in bed?" I inquired. "What's going on, Tati?" Taking my head between his hands – hands usually very warm and pleasant to the touch, but now cold – he said, "Listen, Walti!" I listened intensely to sounds I had never heard before. There was shouting as I had heard it at times coming from drunk folks carousing in an inn. There was the sound of shattering glass punctuated by dull thuds. And what came through very clearly was shrill laughter. I did not understand this hubbub. Also, smoke and a putrid smell were in the air. *Do people get drunk that early in the morning?* I asked myself. "What's going on, Tati, tell me?" Confident as always that my father, the smartest of all people on earth, would know, I was convinced this time also that Tati would have the answer. "Walti," he responded quietly and in a shaky voice, "I think they are burning our synagogue." I felt his cold hands patting my head. Particles of gray ash were settling in my black hair.

At that point the first rays of the rising sun came peeking over the neighbors' roofs. It was a pretty sight. Turning my face up toward my father's, I said, "Look Tati, the sun is rising." To this my father responded with, "Yes, Walti, the sun is rising, but our sun is setting."

Later that morning we walked the four blocks to the synagogue. My father unfortunately had been right once again. The synagogue building lay in ruins with only portions of the red brick walls still erect. The high vertical stained glass windows lay smashed in the street: a lot of broken glass. On the inside, as far as we could ascertain, all was destroyed: the pews, the carpeting, the holy ark that housed the Torah scrolls, the banisters of the gallery. The gallery itself where the women sat had crashed down and lay there twisted on the other burned rubble. Acrid smoke was rising from the smoldering debris. The once beautiful building was utterly ruined.

As we stood there, a few people walked by. Some made an effort not to see the catastrophic sight. Others smiled, made muffled remarks

*My first love and tragedy*

to one another. Still others paused in their walk, took stock of what happened, and shook their heads in disbelief. No one, I remember, spoke to my father, something heretofore never experienced, because in any gathering of people in our town my father had always been recognized and respectfully greeted. Later on that day someone called on the telephone and informed my father that the beautiful, ornate, old synagogue across the river, in what had been Cieszyn before the German occupation, had suffered the same lot the previous night. It too had been irreparably destroyed. The wanton destruction of our places of worship signaled the beginning of the walk through the valley of suffering and death for our Jewish community.

In 1992 my wife Gail and I visited my native town of Český Těšín and Cieszyn, across the Olza River. We visited the sites of the burnt-out synagogues in both towns. Sadly, on neither site of Nazi desecration and destruction had either the Poles or the Czechs found the decency to mount a plaque of commemoration to alert the visitor that a beautiful synagogue had stood here before the war. On the Czech side the terrain was transformed into a blacktopped basketball court, and on the Polish side the fenced-in terrain was totally overgrown with bushes. Obviously, the powers-that-be preferred not to remember.

\* \* \* \* \* \* \* \* \* \* \* \* \*

The date was 568 B.C. when Jerusalem fell to the Babylonians and the Temple, world Jewry's religious center, was destroyed. Most of the city's population were deported to Babylonia. Psalm 137 makes clear the extent of the devastation and the exiles' grief over the catastrophe. The Psalm also reveals how doggedly the Jews in exile hung on to the remembrance of their holy sanctuary come what may. Jewish history leads us to believe that the second destruction of the Jerusalem Temple, this time by the Romans in the year 70 C.E., took place on the very same date, namely the ninth day of the month of *Av* or *Tisha b'Av*. Although it is impossible to verify whether the synchronicity of the two events is historically correct, Jewish tradition commemorates both destructions on the same date. To this day worshipers sit in their places of worship on the floor, barefoot, and by the dim light shed by candles recite *Eichah*, the biblical Book of Lamentations.

It has always been a struggle for me to identify with the memorializing of a catastrophe that took place two and a half millennia ago. Since then the Jewish people have been plagued with a great many other terribly destructive acts, I told myself, so why concentrate on that one again and again? In a discussion with one of my students several years ago, the young Jewish man offered the suggestion that we should be celebrating rather than bemoaning the destruction of the Jerusalem Temple. Because I was shocked by the brash assertion of the youngster, I challenged him to explain his view. And so he volunteered his explanation: was it not a blessing that mass animal sacrifice, a superstitious act that was understood to atone for one's sins, came to a halt thanks to the Temple's disappearance? Was it not a blessing that the rabbis, in trying to adjust to the new historical situation, came to discern a new and better approach to atone for one's sins and to serve God? From here on, according to Rabbi Yochanan ben Zakkai, atonement for the people's sin would be wrought through *gemilut chasadim* or deeds of loving kindness. The young man had perhaps a point, I had to admit. There are times when professors can learn from students.

It is the commemoration of *Tisha b'Av* that has been symbolic of the many sufferings the Jews have had to endure over many centuries. The lamentations sung are not only reminders of our losses over time, are not only sad remembrances of people who innocently perished; they are also entreaties directed to God – the God who purportedly intervenes in human history when needed – to get involved in our history once again in order to bring an ultimate end to Jewish suffering.

And that, of course, raises the whole issue of what the philosophers and theologians have called "theodicy," the justice of God. Why has there been this continued lack of enforced justice? Why has not this allegedly personal all-benevolent and all-powerful God taken notice of what's going on down here below as he did in ancient Egypt according to the Exodus story? Why has God not intervened in favor of the oppressed? These often desperately posed questions which to this very day remain on our lips, to our chagrin, have gone unanswered.

\* \* \* \* \* \* \* \* \* \* \* \* \*

It was a stroke of bad luck that of all places available in our partially emptied town, the SS installed its central office on the floor just below the one we occupied. The house teemed with black-uniformed men day and night. Daily in our going out and our coming in, we had to pass through crowds of SS men gathered in the mezzanine of the staircase. At the front of their visored black military hats was affixed the silver emblem of a human skull. No wonder then that their activities more often than not resulted in human death. They all wore red armbands marked with a black swastika resting on a white circular background. It was a frightening experience to walk through this crowd of uniformed Nazis on our way to and from our apartment.

It must have been no more than three or four days after the Germans occupied our town that one of these SS men rang our doorbell. After a brief exchange of words with this man in the entrance hall, my father, visibly perturbed, informed my mother that he was to accompany the SS man to a meeting with the German authorities. He embraced my mother in the bedroom, and I saw him hand over to her his gold pocket watch, an act I was to witness many times in days to come. Looking down at the street, I saw father entering a black limousine and riding off with the SS. Watching at the window, all my mother was able to utter was the desperate and by now familiar, *"Ach, Du lieber Gott! Was nun?"* (Oh, dear God! What now?).

Then the waiting game began. After one hour my mother was beside herself. Her eyes fixed on the large pendulum clock above the picture of a stern Beethoven looking down over my parents' double bed. She seemed to count the swings of the pendulum. An eternity seemed to have gone by – three excruciating hours of counting elapsed minutes since my father's departure – when finally we heard the sounds of a car screeching to a stop in the street below and his key turning in the lock of the front door. Tati was back, safe and sound, and to our surprise, there was a smile on his face. In response to a nervous barrage of questions thrown at him by Mutti, Edith and me, he explained. *SS* officer Siebert and he were driven to *Der Brauner Hirsch* (The Brown Stag), one of the better hotels of our town. There they had a long conversation over a couple of glasses of beer which, my father laughingly added, he had to pay for. Oh, those cheapskates! *SS Scharführer* (Section Leader) Siebert relayed the Occupation Authority's desire – a desire to which one had no other choice than to acquiesce, of course – that my father organize and preside over a *Judenrat* (Jewish Council), representing the local Jewry vis-à-vis the German authorities, the *SS* and the *Gestapo* (Secret State Police). Obversely, the German authorities would convey their demands to the *Judenrat* whose obligation would be to disseminate these orders to the Jewish populace by means of correspondence, publicly posted announcements, etc. The Council would be provided by the German authorities with the necessary office space and equipment to enable them to function as efficiently as possible. The *Judenrat* was to be formed within one week and, once organized, its membership (i.e., the names, addresses, etc. of these Jewish functionaries) was to be communicated to *SS Scharführer* Siebert at a designated date and time. I still remember my father's last sentence quite clearly: "Anny," he said, "I told you things would not be as bad as we imagined."

Whether my father honestly meant what he said or whether his words were contrived to comfort his wife, I do not know. If the first case holds true and his words were sincere, I cannot help but be amazed and shocked at my father's naiveté. Highly gifted, intelligent and superbly educated as he was – German culture being his favorite field of study – he may have thought that the Germans would respect him despite his Jewishness. Oddly enough, throughout those three years before our deportation, at the helm of the *Judenrat*, and during the worst crises we faced during this period of time, my father was, in fact, always treated with respect. Many times I heard him being addressed as "Herr Doktor" or "Herr Ziffer" even by *Gestapo* officers. On the other hand, none of this seeming respect hindered the Germans from destroying Teschen's Jewish population in the end.

The *Judenrat* was promptly formed. I don't remember the number of men involved, but my uncle Oscar and my great-uncle Arnold were chosen along with other men in whom my father had confidence to competently fill these sensitive posts.

The *Gestapo* chose a house opposite the now burned-down large Polish synagogue to house the *Judenrat* offices. Previously that had been the home of the Polish synagogue's *shammes* or beadle / lay assistant, Mr. Baer. There were three office rooms downstairs. Upstairs lived Mr. Baer and his brother-in-law Mr. Zimmerspitz, the ex-beadle of the now burned-down Czech synagogue, with their spouses. My father's deputy was a Mr. Loeffler whose son George and I became the *Laufburschen* or messenger boys of the *Judenrat* and best of friends.

The *Gestapo* did not let us wait very long for their first anti-Jewish order, alas. Within one week of the *Judenrat's* existence, posters affixed to houses, fences and special bulletin boards made known the date at which all Jews were obligated to wear white armbands with a blue *Magen David*, the six-pointed Star of David, imprinted on them. I must confess that in my youthful innocence, seeing the posters carrying my father's name made me proud. The two mitigating factors bearing on the presence of my father's name and signature at the bottom of this Nazi edict were the fact that he had no choice in the matter of having his name there and that, fortunately, above his name was the phrase *Im Auftrage der Staatspolizei* ("By order of the Gestapo"). I presume that most of our Jews were fully aware of Nazi coercion that made my father's name appear on that poster. I am supported in this conviction by the fact that at no time did I detect even the least animosity directed against my father by our fellow Jews during those long and miserable three years before our deportation.

It was also around this time that a representative of the *SS* headquarters below our apartment appeared at our door one day and ordered us to vacate the premises within three days. Permission was granted to each one of us to take along a couple of suitcases with our belongings. The rest of the apartment (i.e., the furniture, rugs, library, china, etc.) "will be well taken care of by us," the *SS* man assured us. Oh, what magnanimity!

My mother wept; my father looked grim but said nothing; my sister cursed the *SS* and followed that up with a special curse on Adolf Hitler. During the night, so as to avoid the *SS* men's possible jeering and obstructions, we made our way very quietly out of the house, the house where I had spent the previous twelve years of my life. We moved in with Uncle Oskar, Aunt Else and their daughter Ilse, my cousin and best friend, who lived in an apartment house owned by them three blocks away.

Our stay there was not to last very long. Apart from the constant clashes Mutti had with Aunt Else over the use of the kitchen and bathroom, I remember especially one unpleasant incident not related to these women's personal feuding. Goebbels, the *Reich* propaganda minister who exceeded most of his government peers in rabid antisemitism, came to town. There was a rally in his honor during which he, as could be expected, vituperated against the Jews who worked toward the destruction of Germany and all cultured Aryan nations and therefore had to be destroyed. It took place almost under our windows, in Goethe Street, which led to the large plaza in front

## *My first love and tragedy*

of our town office building. Edith, Ilse and I stood behind closed windows watching the spectacle of several thousands of the town's population cheering and applauding. When the rally ended and the people were dismissed, many of them exited from the plaza through our street. We were spotted at the window, and within a few minutes the stones started flying, one of which hit and shattered the glass panes. Fortunately, we had just enough time to retreat to the inside of the room, and so no one was hurt.

A few days later we were evicted from there as well.

Two further evictions followed until we all ended up in a ghetto on the outskirts of our town, in an area called *Der Boberhügel*, the site of a very large abandoned farm complex with various outbuildings. The center of this ghetto consisted of several dance halls which, when divided into compartments each measuring about ten by ten feet by sheets hanging from suspended wires, provided the lodging for the various family units. The stage area of one of the halls housed three such units, with our family occupying the middle one.

This was a precarious time, to be sure, but life went on among the nine hundred and some Jews of our town. For me, at least one part of this miserable existence brought unprecedented happiness: I fell in love with Lydia. I met her in the ghetto over an improvised ping-pong table and for me it was love at first sight and for the first time. I was thirteen. She was fourteen. Her large green smiling eyes mesmerized me. Her golden hair, tied in a thick braid, those lovely eyes, the scent I inhaled passing by her as we changed sides during the game, her well-developed body, all these drew me to her with a magnetism I, a very shy boy, would never have thought possible before. Lydia responded to her continued losing streaks with bright laughter that sounded like the tinkling of silver bells. She was truly a lovely young woman, and I knew with absoluteness that I must get to know her better. This was bliss.

The opportunity soon offered itself. Knowing that employment in a German war-related industry postponed deportation, my father succeeded in procuring for our town's young Jewish people jobs on the night shift in a nut-and-bolt factory in the nearby town of Freistadt. And so every afternoon around three p.m. we set out toward the train station to board a train. The trip took about one hour, and the factory itself was within easy walking distance from the station. Imagine my surprise when I sat down on an empty compartment bench – and Lydia chose to sit down next to me. Other empty seats were available, but she happened to pick me to sit next to. This happened several times and boded well for the future, I thought. During the half hour around midnight that was allotted to us for eating our snacks, Lydia and I sat apart from the others, and ate our sandwiches and fruits. And then, during one of the night train rides, as we sat next to each other, I mustered all my courage and slid my hand into hers. My happiness was complete when she held on to my hand with her warm hand and smilingly looked at me. Words do not suffice to express how love-smitten I now was. This first manifestation of our shared love was from here on repeated daily. But now, in addition to holding hands, we leaned against each other with our cheeks touching and burning. Oh, how I wished the train ride would last forever. On weekends Lydia and I strolled through the few meadows surrounding the ghetto that were allowed to us. We knew we were under the German guards' eyes, of course, but we were thankful for not being molested by them. The ones that did molest us on some of these innocent walks were Polish peasant boys. I remember a number of times when these rough fellows walked by us as we sat in the grass and, grinning, said to me, "Man, why don't you fuck her? What are you waiting for?" Blood shot to our cheeks, and we pretended not to have heard those words.

Despite the many hardships we experienced, this was a glorious time for me. Not only was I in love for the first time, but given my interest in mechanical things I actually enjoyed the work at the nut-and-bolt factory. Working on large lathes, cutting threads into bolts used for connecting rails and other heavy machinery applications, having to adjust and sharpen the cutters every so often with wrenches and special tools, added to my desire to learn more about things mechanical and my determination to become a mechanical engineer once the war came to an end and we were free.

In one of the open sheds of the ghetto farm stood an old jalopy pickup truck. With a few German *Marks* saved up from filing house keys for some of our people, I had bought myself a set of wrenches. Equipped with these, I set out to dismantle the engine of that old truck. I needed to know what a cylinder, a piston, a valve and a carburetor looked like and how they functioned. I must have taken that old carburetor apart a dozen times, proudly explaining to my parents and sister how all this worked. But that fun came to an end when one day Schaeffer, a *Gestapo* man, came to search our living quarters. He found my beloved set of wrenches and simply took them. When my mother implored him not to deprive me of these tools which I had very arduously acquired, he laughed into her face and responded with a single word: *"Quatsch!"* – the equivalent to our "Crap!" Taking stock of the rest of our belongings, he noticed father's two cameras on a shelf. Turning to my parents with a sarcastic smile, he said, "Well, well, what a happy coincidence! My little boy has his birthday next week. These cameras will make a lovely birthday present for him." Snatching the two cameras, he walked out of the room.

My first-love euphoria ended when one evening Lydia, with tears in her eyes, informed me that her parents, Mr. and Mrs. Rindl, decided to clandestinely escape from the ghetto. Their plan was to flee the German-occupied territory toward the Soviet Union which was then seen as a haven for Jews. When the time came to say goodbye, Lydia unfastened her gold necklace and handed to me a little gold pendant consisting of a yoke and a round little disc held in between which, when spun, spelled out the words "I love you" in English. Her last words to me were, "As you spin this little disc you will remember me and our love for each other. Guard it well, until we see each other again." We embraced and she, with tears running down her cheeks, quietly left. The time to see each other again unfortunately never came. A couple of weeks later my father was informed that the bodies of the Rindl family were discovered some fifty kilometers east of our town. All three of them had been shot dead. A German patrol had apparently intercepted and murdered them on the spot. I was heartbroken.

There is a sequel to this story. A few years ago, after I had shared my Holocaust experiences with an audience of high school teachers in Maine, one of the ladies approached me. Drawing from her pocket a small item, she handed it to me and asked, "Is this the kind of pendant Lydia gave you before leaving the ghetto?" To my amazement this was a cheap but exact metal replica of the gold pendant Lydia had given me many decades earlier. This lady teacher had attended one of my lectures a few years earlier and had heard my story then. She had never forgotten it. Years later she found the small item at a flea market. In a flash she remembered my story of Lydia and promised herself to give the replica of this little token of Lydia's love to me in appreciation for my sharing the story with others. I was deeply moved by this gesture of compassion. To this day the little pendant she gave me accompanies me everywhere I go in my key wallet. It has traveled with me for many years, as has the remembrance of Lydia, the beautiful, golden-haired, green-eyed girl I loved.

Soon after hearing about Lydia's death, our lives ominously changed. The work at the factory was abruptly cancelled, and my father had the premonition that deportation was imminent. We called it "deportation" while the Germans, great masters of dissimulation and lies, called it *Umsiedlung nach Osten* or "resettlement to the East."

Tati was right. On June 28, 1942, we were informed through loudspeakers mounted to trucks circling the ghetto that each person was to have one suitcase packed and ready the following morning.

Mother packed what she considered the most important items for each of us. Making these decisions was excruciatingly difficult.

## *My first love and tragedy*

After all, we had not the slightest idea what our destination would be and what would await us there. Surely we would have to perform some kind of work there, but what? What was the climate like that awaited us? Perhaps more importantly still, would we as a family remain together or would there be separation? I still hear my mother moaning and imploring our *lieber Gott* to help and protect us and, most of all, to keep us together. My father looked grim and said nothing. My sister cursed the Nazis as usual.

The next morning things happened as announced. From the different farm buildings emerged men, women and children, each carrying one suitcase. This mass of people, numbering just under one thousand, marched, accompanied on each side by SS men, to the *Sammelplatz* or assembly place. The latter was a defunct junkyard close to the town's railroad station. Behind a long row of tables sat SS men. In front of each one of them lay a leather whip and a hand gun. As we processed by, one by one, the Germans barked at us to hand over all our valuables. I do not remember whether my parents had anything to hand over. When it was my turn, I boldly said, "I have nothing." Instinctively I refused to hand over to those thugs the much coveted Omega steel pocket watch my father had given me on my previous birthday.

Every so often a man or woman would be pulled from the long line of these frightened people and taken into a small barrack nearby. We then heard screams. The barrack door would fly open shortly after, and the poor man or woman would literally be kicked out. I especially remember one man landing on the ground with his head bloodied. Never had I seen such a terrifying sight before. It scared me out of my wits, and that never-handed-over Omega watch of mine seemed to burn a hole in my pocket.

After the people had passed by the tables, men and women were separated. My father and mother were directed to join groups of middle-aged folk of their respective sexes, my sister was herded toward a young women's group, and I was pushed toward a group of boys. I knew some of these youngsters from our common work at the nut-and-bolt factory.

Let me mention at this point that out of the group of fifteen boys about my age whom I knew, only two survived the Holocaust: Peter Berger, who after the war emigrated to Israel, and I.

I now became increasingly worried about not having handed over the Omega pocket watch. After mulling this over and realizing the danger I would be in if found out, I dug a shallow hole in the ground with the heel of my shoe. Most carefully, so as not to be seen by anyone, I lowered the watch by its chain into the hole, covering it with dirt and carefully marking the place by placing a distinctive piece of junk iron over it. The rusty old gear, I was certain, would help me identify the spot in the future. I felt relieved to have gotten rid of the watch whose discovery on me could have jeopardized my life. Also the realization that I had outwitted the Germans gave me a feeling of satisfaction. In the end, I said to myself, I'd be back shortly and then reclaim my rightful possession.

Trains began arriving. The SS herded people into the railroad cars. I heard the word *schneller* (faster) again and again, something I would have to get used to in days to come. Then it was our turn.

Two things from that fateful event stand out for me: the separation from my parents and sister, and the chaos created by the guards. We had never been apart from each other before during the fifteen years of my life. When I was pointed toward the group of youngsters and was forced to leave my family, my mother ran after me. Reaching out to me and weeping, she uttered "Walti! Walti!" An SS man with his whip slapped her on the head. Shouting "enough of that" and pulling her back by her clothes, he pushed her toward the group she was to join. It is beyond me today, as father of four children of my own, to even vaguely imagine what my mother and so many other parents must have gone through that day. The other things that stand out for me in retrospect are the shouting, the rough commands, the dogs barking and straining at their leashes, and the hapless faces of the victims in their total disorientation at a complete loss as to what to do. This was utter mayhem, and it was intentionally produced by the Nazis. I witnessed this kind of chaos over and over again during the three years I was to spend in German slave labor camps. It is absolutely true that there was in our persecutors something akin to joy in the bestial treatment they handed out to their victims. In Daniel Goldhagen's book *Hitler's Willing Executioners*, the word "willing" is an understatement. The men and women to whom this adjective applies seemed to derive outright pleasure and satisfaction from torturing and murdering people.

Once loaded on the trains, we were off to a destination unknown. Despite the many young people around me, I felt terribly alone and scared. Clutching the little pendant Lydia had given me, I felt hot tears running down my cheeks.

When the train came to a stop, we were again chaotically unloaded in the railroad station of the city of Sosnowitz (Polish: Sosnowiec) in former Upper Polish Silesia. There, after being counted a number of times, we were marched through the town to a large, probably four-story-high building named Dulag, short for German *Durchgangslager* or "transit camp." Once in the building, each one of us was assigned a bunk, a designated portion of a wooden platform equipped with a burlap sack filled with straw.

I do not remember the length of time we stayed in the *Dulag*. It must have been several days. The work assignments in the *Dulag* were minor ones dealing with the cleaning and maintenance of the building itself. We were largely left alone. In the morning, at noon, and around five in the afternoon the call *Antreten* (assemble) was announced. Herded down to the courtyard by the *Kapos* (camp police consisting of prisoners), the ritual was always the same: counting by the *Kapos* and distribution of meager food rations. At first I could not get myself to eat that miserable bowl of soup at noon. I offered it to an older inmate; he hastily grabbed it and slurped it down. But before long, as hunger set in, I not only impatiently looked forward to the moments of food distribution, but when they came, hungrily gobbled up every bit of it.

It was also at noon, during these assemblies, that mail was distributed to the prisoners. It was on such an occasion that I received my first letter from my parents, informing me that they, too, were now in Sosnowitz and were trying hard to get Edith, my cousin Ilse, and me released from the *Dulag*. The "superior *Judenrat*" for all of Silesia was located in Sosnowitz, and a Jew by the name of Moshe Merin, its chairperson under whose umbrella organization my father had chaired the local *Judenrat* of Teschen, was kindly disposed to my father. Thus Edith, Ilse and I had every reason to believe that my father, who now worked in Merin's offices, would be successful in getting us released. As a matter of fact, it was during the noon assembly that every so often the names of certain prisoners were called out, after which these lucky folks were allowed to fetch their suitcases and then happily marched out of the *Dulag* through the courtyard gate into the street where family and friends jubilantly welcomed them.

One night I woke up to a commotion taking place on the floor below us. Silently I crawled down from my top bunk located on the fourth floor to investigate what was going on below. As I carefully peeked around the corner, I saw prisoners in blue and white striped prison garb carry in stretchers loaded with people and deposit them in the long hall. After hauling in the last of perhaps twenty-five such stretchers, the carriers disappeared and gave me an opportunity to approach a bit closer. What I saw frightened me beyond description. On the stretchers lay men who no longer looked like living human beings: emaciated, with protruding large eyes, no hair on their skulls, their mouths often wide open, some devoid of teeth, moaning and groaning, uttering words I could not understand, shapes that reminded me of illustrations of the grim reaper I had seen in some of my father's books. The scene I witnessed that night I will never forget. What haunted me most were these men's eyes which seemed to look straight at me without being able to see me, those eyes devoid of all expression. Total emptiness. There was groaning – terrible sounds that defy description. And there was also the stench of filth and decay.

Hearing an approaching noise in the corridor, I quickly stole back to my hall above and crawled back into the bunk. I lay there for quite a while trying to figure out who these people were and from where they may have come. But the secret defied a solution, and I finally fell asleep. Come next morning, the stretchers with these frightful, no longer human apparitions had vanished, and I thought it best to keep that night's adventure to myself. Hell must be peopled by figures like these, I thought to myself.

A few days later, during the noon ritual, the names of my sister and cousin were called out. With just enough time to bid me tearfully goodbye, they hastily assured me they would prod my father into doing his utmost for my release. Then, with suitcases in hand, they marched out the gate into what turned out to be temporary freedom.

That afternoon I stood at one of the windows on the fourth floor wistfully looking down on the street below. I had hoped that my parents would show up as they had several times before to offer me some assurance, some sign of hope by their presence. In my hand I held a small piece of paper, now crumpled into a little ball, ready to be thrown down to the street if and when my parents showed up. On that piece of paper I implored them to get me out of the *Dulag*. Especially after seeing the terrible sights on the stretchers the night before, I was in despair. When my parents did show up under the windows, I threw that little ball of paper down to them. I saw them fetch it and read it down in the street. I saw my mother reaching for her handkerchief and dabbing her eyes. My father motioned to me as if to say, "I tried everything but was not successful. Don't give up,

Walti! We will continue our effort to free you."

Tears flooded my eyes as I realized the hopelessness of my situation. Everything became blurred as my parents and Edith threw me kisses, slowly turned and disappeared from sight.

Two days later my young friends and I were taken to the Sosnowitz station and loaded onto trains.

CHAPTER 6
# Initiation into hell: Sakrau

The train started rolling, leaving Sosnowitz quickly behind. There were a lot of scared youngsters on the train, and there was no one to reassure or to give advice.

More than once on that train churning eastward did I pray to the *lieber Gott* whom my mother always spoke about so lovingly, the *lieber Gott* who, this time again, did not show up to deliver us children, or better, "his" children, from evil. While I clutched Lydia's pendant in my cold hand I was, at least for a short while, transported back in time when life was beautiful.

There was silence in the railroad car but for the muffled noise of weeping children.

This was not a long ride, at the most two hours or so. None of my friends recognized the area through which the train was taking us. And no wonder! Few of us had ever ventured beyond a few miles from our home towns and villages. The train came to a halt in a place by the name of Sakrau. We saw the name inscribed on the train station.

Here at the Sakrau camp began the hellish series of seven slave camps in all, ending on May 8, 1945, with my liberation by the Soviet army in the concentration camp of Waldenburg, a sub-camp belonging to the Gross-Rosen group of camps located south of the then German city of Breslau which, after the war, became Wrocław and part of Poland.

Because my intention is to write a memoir dealing with the totality of my life up to this moment, it will be impossible to describe in detail my various experiences in those seven concentration camps. I will limit myself to moments that stand out from the rest of this utterly bleak, dreary, miserable and dangerous existence that I was forced to live for nearly three years. These selected moments will convey the utter physical and mental degradation inflicted upon us by the despicable Nazi overlords.

With Sakrau began a three-year-long period of being shuffled from one camp to the next approximately every six months. The lack of calendars, of contact with the outside world, of any knowledge of what was going on beyond the triple fences of the camps, accounted for our living in a timeless kind of limbo.

After surviving the chaotic arrival ritual at the railway station with its shouting, pushing, whipping by both *SS* and *Kapos*, and the barking and snapping of dogs, we began marching to the camp in sweltering heat. The guards, perhaps from innate meanness or from their desire to get this over with and get to their quarters, rushed us on, making generous use of their whips and rifle butts. It was not long before I saw one of the prisoners throw away his suitcase. At the tempo of the march that was forced upon us, it was virtually impossible to schlep the valises. Within a few minutes all our suitcases lay in the ditches and with them the last material connections to our previous state of relative freedom and family. We arrived in camp devoid of any personal possessions other than the clothes on our backs.

Every day from here on became a challenge to one's ingenuity for survival. As a fifteen-year-old, I had to learn quickly from some of the more seasoned prisoners. While with my five foot five inch build I have always been short, I was muscular and strong. That helped. It may have been my upbringing that instilled in me a serious work

## Initiation into hell: Sakrau

ethic. I still hear my father say to me, "Walti, when you do something, whatever it may be, do it right."

To practice a good work ethic in a concentration camp may not have been the wisest thing to do for obvious reasons. But I was only fifteen and so, commandeered to work in a sand quarry, loading construction-type lorries (German: *Kipwagen*), my zeal to do good work got the better of me. Sending shovels full of moist sand through the air, without that sand breaking up and scattering, gave me a certain satisfaction. And so I shoveled assiduously and, as a result, filled my lorry faster than the others. My naive work ethic necessarily reflected negatively on the others' work.

It wasn't long before my fellow workers, aware of my stupidly applied zeal, strongly disapproved of what I was doing. On a foggy morning when visibility was poor, I suddenly found myself knocked down onto the sand and pummeled by fellow prisoners. I did not understand what had happened. Back in camp I naively inquired of one of my attackers why they had done this to me. The response came quickly and cogently, "When the guards watch, you shovel. When the guards look away, you stop working. You want to survive, don't you?" I had learned my lesson. But I must admit that I did not like what I was told. I would have preferred throwing those wet clumps of sand into the lorry as I had before, faster and more artfully than the others. As a result of this incident some of my fellow Jewish prisoners gave me the not so flattering epithet "*Jaecke*," a word whose connotation was "dumb German." As a fellow Jew and prisoner I strongly resented this appellation. It hurt.

It occurred to me at the time that some of the resentment expressed toward me came also from my inability to converse with my fellow Jews in their language, Yiddish. The tongue spoken in our home was German, *Hochdeutch* (high German), albeit with a Slavic accent. And so from this incident on I tried very hard to acquire a Yiddish vocabulary and, most importantly, Yiddish idioms. Cursing the Germans in Yiddish, I hoped, would give me a better chance to be socially accepted by these Polish Jews.

Perhaps it was thanks to my ability to send the sand so efficiently into the lorries that I was "promoted" to be an assistant to a locomotive driver who pulled the filled lorries to their destination where they were dumped. This process widened the future roadbed for the *Autobahn*, the new auto expressway, the construction of which was started under Hitler's regime. The locomotive driver was a Pole of impressive physique.

Far from being a promotion or a betterment of my situation, working for that Pole was hell. My job consisted of neatly stacking pressed coal dust cubes called briquettes around the boiler of the locomotive, and to run ahead of the machine to throw the rail switches at certain places of the itinerary. This work was physically less challenging than shoveling sand all day. But there was a recurring problem that when the locomotive began pulling the heavy filled lorries, this resulted in shaking and jerking as the wheels madly turned, seeking sufficient friction to haul the load. The jerking action regularly demolished my artful stacking of the coal briquettes. Portions of the stacks around the boiler collapsed, some falling on the huge Pole's boots. There was nothing that could be done to prevent this, but the antisemitic Polish colossus didn't know better than to blame me for the mishap. Pushing me into the corner of the cab, he slapped my face and kicked me, calling me a dirty Jew who was good for nothing. On one such occasion he pushed me off the locomotive and steamed away, forcing me to run quite a distance behind the train. I eventually overtook the locomotive as it slowed and managed to throw the proper switch. While watching me in my dilemma, the huge sadistic Pole bellowed with laughter. When I regained the steps of the locomotive, he said to me threateningly, "Next time, you stupid Jew, I'll run over you and haul you back stretched out on the bumpers. The Germans surely won't mind." After one other of these unavoidable fiascos with the coal briquettes, the brute must have asked for another prisoner to work with, because I saw myself demoted to shoveling sand in the quarry.

In Sakrau it was still minimally possible to communicate with the outside world. Once, a locomotive mechanic called me aside. "Tonight after supper, walk along such and such a side of the fence. And be there alone." I followed his advice and that evening, as I stood there, half a loaf of bread was thrown to me across the fence. When with my newly acquired treasure I arrived at the barrack and began breaking the bread apart to share some of it with my fellow prisoners, I found a little note embedded in the bread. It was from my father. In a few terse sentences he reassured me that he continued trying to get me set free and that Mr. Merin himself was involved in the effort. "Don't give up hope, Walti," he wrote. "We all think of you constantly and we love you."

Chewing this dark bread and realizing that my mother had probably baked it herself, perhaps with me in mind, helped me feel a little bit less abandoned. My friends marveled, "Your dad sure must have important connections." From this moment on my relationship with the others improved. No longer was I called "*Jaecke.*" I was now one of them.

CHAPTER 7
# In the midst of hell: Brande

On innumerable occasions after sharing my stories with others, I have been asked, "But why did they transfer you from camp to camp so often?" I have no answer to that question. We do know, however, based on post-war German documentation, that the Nazis awarded priority to Jewish prisoner transfers over critical strategic movement of military personnel and materiel. The Germans clearly suffered from a psychosis in which the elimination of Jews constituted their program's highest priority.

My time in the camp of Sakrau came to an end when one day at the morning roll call the much-dreaded *soykher* appeared. The Yiddish term stands for "salesman" because like a salesman trading his wares, this SS officer transferred human ware – Jewish prisoners – from one camp to another. As it happened, I was one of the selected Jews, and this meant that my time in Sakrau was up. With it disappeared the rare but occasional blessing of receiving bits of information embedded in loaves of bread. My contact with family from here on was definitively lost.

A convoy of military trucks took us to the Sakrau station where we were herded into cattle cars without any provisions for the trip. Squeezed together like sardines in standing position in mid-winter, we were extremely lucky that the train ride did not last long. When we arrived and had survived the dangerous chaotic arrival ritual, undoubtedly orchestrated to intimidate us both physically and mentally, we began marching through the snow. This time there were no suitcases to drag along.

I remember the stillness of the countryside clothed in white. I will never forget the feeling of abandonment as I noticed little houses here and there, at considerable distance, jotting out from the snowy landscape with little lights shining in their windows. It occurred to me then that it must be Christmas time, and these little lights were Christmas tree lights. I realized that six months had gone by since my separation from my parents. This was one of those last rare times when I still recalled the past, a luxury which from here on began gradually disappearing.

Christmas-Hanukkah memories overwhelmed me. My parents were not religious Jews. While we lit the traditional Hanukkah lights, eight with the servant-candle, the *shammes*, making nine, we also had a nicely decorated Christmas tree in our living room. By having one, I wonder whether my parents wanted to accommodate our Roman Catholic Slovak maid and cook Malci Kurjan, who had her own little room in the apartment next to the kitchen and who after many years of service had become part of our family. Edith and I considered her very much a second mother.

It was under the Christmas tree that we found our gifts and not during the eight days of Hanukkah. This is how assimilation had transformed us. Decades later when I lived in Bangor, Maine, Hershel, an immigrant from Eastern Europe and one of Beth Israel synagogue's members, said when introduced to me, "Oh, so you hail from that part of Czechoslovakia where the Jews were known to have problems. You know what I mean, don't you?" I immediately understood what this orthodox old Jew meant when, with this quasi-polite term "problem," he suggested that back then already we were known as Jews who had strayed from traditional Judaism.

## In the midst of hell: Brande

And so we marched through the night. We heard the bells from some close village steeples ring out, and that reminded me of the many church bells, from both Catholic and Protestant church steeples, that had rung out the hours in my hometown of Teschen and which in unison had called the population to worship on Sunday mornings. I felt terribly sad trudging through the snow with wonderful memories from past years, from past Christmases, inundating my mind.

The snow crunched under our feet for about forty-five minutes before we arrived at the gates of slave labor camp Brande, a camp whose memory would never leave me. Brande bored itself into my psyche like no other camp, before or after. After the war my sister informed me that they were tremendously relieved when finding out that I had been sent to Brande. My sister, at the time still in Sosnowitz and working as a secretary in the *Dulag*, had access to information regarding the whereabouts of the prisoners who had passed through the *Dulag*. Brande, it seems, was known as an *Erholungslager*, a convalescence camp, for tired prisoners who needed rest before being sent back to work. And it is true, there was no work to be done in Brande other than the necessary activities to keep the camp clean and functioning. In Brande, my sister thought, I would be spared from back-breaking and exhausting physical work prisoners were exposed to elsewhere. Jubilantly she announced one day to my parents, "Walti is in Brande! What a blessing!"

Little did she and the outside world know what really went on in Brande. Far from being a convalescence camp, prisoners in Brande were murdered daily to the enjoyment of the German camp commander whose name was Kurt Bruno Pompe.

Brande was a relatively small camp with wooden barracks surrounding the central grassy rectangle that was crisscrossed by several gravel walkways. To one side of the entrance gates stood the camp office with the adjacent refectory barrack; farther back was a shed set aside for the preparation of vegetables such as potato and beet peeling done by the prisoners, a much-coveted job; and around the corner from there stood the wash barracks on a slightly elevated ground. The rest of the barracks surrounded concentrically the central assembly grounds. Each barrack held several rooms equipped with three-tier high bunks, each equipped with a burlap sack filled with straw.

After our arrival within the camp, late at night, there was the usual headcount by the German camp guards and the *Kapos* under command of the *Lagerälteste* or camp eldest, a tall Jewish man clad in something resembling a gray Eisenhower jacket, black riding pants and black, knee-high boots. His was a ruddy coarse face with a large protruding red nose. Ugly. In his hand he held an all-leather, black-jack-like club, which he constantly beat against his boots, producing a sound resembling the strong claps of hands. Standing in the middle of the assembly square, he shouted out commands to his *Kapo* assistants, alternating between Polish and heavily accented German.

The headcount completed, we were driven to the wash barracks. There, to my frustration, we had to undress completely. Standing in the nude in front of the camp barbers, our head hair was clipped to a length of about one-eighth of an inch, and then a one-inch wide stripe was shaved running from the front to the back of our heads. Another barber, in the meantime, was taking care of our armpits and genital areas. The next one brushed a liquid on the shaven body areas which, within a few moments, burned the living daylights out of us. The affected areas of our skin turned ruby red. Herded into the shower room, we were then drenched with lukewarm water. The few towels provided to us and shared by a number of prisoners helped us dry just sufficiently to allow us to slip into our old clothes and shoes. The *Kapos* who constantly hurried us on then drove us like cattle to the barracks and our respective *Stuben*, or rooms.

Once in the room, each one of us was assigned a bunk area and two blankets. One of these was to envelop the burlap sack filled with straw that waited for us there, the other to cover ourselves with.

## In the midst of hell: Brande

Hastily I draped the gray thin blanket around my burlap sack, pulled the other blanket up to my chin, and, totally exhausted, fell asleep.

I woke the next morning to the disturbing sound of someone hitting the wooden bunks with a leather knout and shouting *"Raus aus den Betten!"* "Out of the beds! Quick! Wash! Assemble at the whistle!" Following everybody's rush to the wash barracks, I managed barely to wet my hands and face and, at the *Kapos*' whistle, to arrive at the assembly square for the roll call where *Kapos* arranged us into rows five deep. In retrospect, it seems to me that there must have been between five hundred and six hundred prisoners standing there.

Then came the shout *Achtung!*, at which we came to attention. The gates of the camp opened, and in came limping a man dressed in a dark brown uniform. This was German camp commandant Pompe. As I was told later, his uniform was that of a member of the *Organization Todt*, a German military unit equivalent to our Corps of Engineers. Clearly, all the German slave labor camps and later concentration camps were not administered by the *SS*.

Pompe limped. Later I was told that he had lost the lower part of his right leg in World War I combat on the western front. The first impression I got was that he strongly resembled Hitler. I well remember his ashen gray wrinkled face, his Hitler-like mustache, his harsh voice with which I was to become quite familiar in Schmiedeberg, a camp I was transferred to later.

At the shout of *Achtung!*, the *Lagerälteste* or prisoner commandant of the camp and the *Kapos* snapped to attention. The former then marched up to Pompe and, facing him, gave a report on the status of the camp, the new arrivals from last night, etc. Pompe nodded his head in agreement and then proceeded to inspect us, slowly walking through our ranks and looking each one of us intensely in the face. The process was totally unnerving.

Having inspected us from close up, Pompe left the camp to the repeated shout of *Achtung!* This was followed by the appearance of the

Jewish office personnel to whom we were ordered to give our names, city or village of provenance, and age. The Jewish camp commander, Mr. Gebuehrer, listened to this litany of information. Every so often he interjected a question or made a remark. Then it was my turn. After I gave my name, Mr. Gebuehrer walked up to me and asked, "Are you by any chance the son of Dr. Ziffer the attorney from Teschen?" To which I answered, "Yes, he is my father, sir." Placing his arm on my shoulder, he pulled me out of the rank of prisoners and walked with me to his room, a small private room, at the end of one of the barracks.

He bade me sit down in a chair and told me that he knew my father, who had at one time represented him in a litigation trial. Gebuehrer told me that he hailed from the city of Bielitz (previously Polish Bielsko), a town in Poland some thirty miles northeast of my town of Teschen. Because I came from such a fine family, he said, he would make me his personal attendant and help me.

My job, beginning the next day, would be making a fire in his wood stove early in the morning. I would have to polish his boots, clean his room, and bring his food from the refectory at noon and in the evening. There would be other chores from time to time, of which he would inform me. With his boot he then kicked open a large wooden crate under his table and said, "*Mein Kleiner* (my little one), feel free to help yourself to the food that's in there anytime." Glancing into the box I saw loose pieces of bread, sandwiches and packages that had not yet been opened. Then, opening the door to one of his cupboards, he pointed to jars of preserves and honey and packets of sugar. "If I ever catch you helping yourself to these, I am done with you. Do you understand, *mein Kleiner*?" And after a brief pause he added in a rather menacing tone, "What's under the table is yours. But don't dare taking any of it to your barrack!" Needless to say, I was overjoyed to have found such a generous protector in Mr. Gebuehrer.

Many years later, surfing the Internet, I found a website of the post-war Jewish community of Bielsko. On the spur of the moment

## In the midst of hell: Brande

I inquired after the fate of Mr. Gebuehrer. They responded that no such person was known to them nor had they found that name on the surviving lists of the pre-war Jewish community. And so the provenance of this Mr. Gebuehrer remains for me a complete mystery to this day.

The following morning I began my special duties very early, a *Kapo* having waked me for that purpose. Everything went satisfactorily. Then came the whistles for the roll call at which, despite my privileged new position, I had to participate.

The previous morning's ritual repeated itself with one significant difference: when Pompe mustered us this this time, he selected about a dozen prisoners by tapping them on the head with his whip, at which they had to step out from their rank and form a separate small party. Accompanied by *Kapos*, they were marched off to the wash barrack and we, other prisoners, were dismissed. Shortly after, terrifying screaming, howling, piercing cries and shrill shouting emanated from there. Gradually the noise abated until all was still again. Under the constant eyes of the *Kapos*, I dared not inquire about the cause for this alarming noise, and I continued my work shoveling snow in a corner of the camp. When I finally returned to my room, I was appalled at what I saw.

A number of young people standing at one end of a lower bunk were masturbating. A piece of paper was spread on the blanket. The one whose ejaculate spurted out the farthest was applauded by the rest of the boys and after several such contests was declared the winner. As could be expected, I was immediately invited to participate in this contest, but I politely declined, finding this whole activity disgusting. I also felt, relatively small that I was, that I was no match for some of these tall young fellows. Once again I felt isolated and alienated from my fellow inmates whose ethnic and cultural background was so very different from mine.

Later that same day, I turned to several older inmates. To my question concerning the terrifying noise emanating from the wash barracks that morning, they looked at me silently as if to say, "So you can't figure this out yourself, you little idiot," and walked away without responding. I could have asked Mr. Gebuehrer, of course, but I did not have the courage to do so.

The answer to my puzzlement about the terrifying noises came soon enough, though. A few days later, my work of cleaning the camp grounds was interrupted by *Kapos* who had rounded up another two boys already. The three of us were taken to the wash barracks that late morning, and what we saw defies description. There, on the tiled floor in the midst of blood, body fluids and excrement, lay a dozen nude bodies in various states of convulsion. These were shapes that refuse verbal representation. Any attempt at description would be an understatement of the horror I witnessed. For lack of any better comparison, I can only think of store window mannequins whose arms, legs and neck had been twisted out of shape into bizarre new configurations and all this sprinkled and stained with blood and filth.

Our job was to clean up these chunks of inanimate flesh which only a few hours before had been thinking and breathing human beings. A two-wheeled cart was provided at the rear of the barrack. On it we loaded the distorted corpses of our fellow prisoners and carted them into the nearby woods where we dumped them into a deep mass grave. There they rejoined previous victims similarly murdered. Then we returned to the barrack and cleaned it up. Never in my life had I seen the result of such an orgy of violence. Witnessing this devastation was the beginning of my descent toward loss of personhood, an abyss planned and executed by Hitler's willing torturers and executioners. But what had been the method of murder of these victims, I asked myself again and again. I found out later that the torture and eventual death of these unfortunates was brought about by Pompe himself, the guards and some *Kapos*, who showered their victims with ice cold water and alternately poured over them boiling water taken from the kettles used for washing the German personnel's laundry,

## In the midst of hell: Brande

located in that same barrack. In between the terrible water treatment, the prisoners were assaulted with whips, rifle butts, kicks and beatings, until they mercifully expired. After letting me in on this secret, the men nodded their heads and, looking at me with an incredibly sad expression, whispered, "Now you know."

"Will it be me tomorrow morning?" must have been many a man's frightening last thought before falling asleep. But I felt relatively safe, telling myself that Mr. Gebuehrer had promised me protection. Surely Pompe must have been told about my special relationship with the camp eldest and he would abstain from selecting me. This thought spurred me on to do the special work for Mr. Gebuehrer as conscientiously as possible.

My sister, back in Sosnowitz, rejoiced upon seeing on a report that I had been taken to Brande, the convalescence camp, as I mentioned before. A scribe in the camp office named Bornstein seems to have known about the misconception about Brande circulating among the Jews still living in the ghetto, and he tried to clear this up by smuggling a letter out of the camp. In this letter he explained the real state of affairs in Brande and how Pompe methodically murdered the prisoners. This letter, at one point, was intercepted. What followed began with a loud speaker call for me to come to the refectory barrack. Mr. Gebuehrer and a number of *Kapos* were already there as I hastily entered. Shortly after, Pompe himself arrived. As we all stood there, Bornstein was brought in under escort. He was a young man, somewhere in his middle twenties, short and stocky. His large, myopic, bulgy eyes looked at us through a pair of thick glasses. He walked in upright and seemingly fearless although he may have been expecting something ominous to happen.

Pompe now approached him with a vile smile that distorted his already ugly face into an utterly mean grimace. Brandishing in his hand a piece of paper, he shouted, "You piece of shit, Bornstein, did you try to smuggle this letter out of the camp?" To this the young man silently nodded agreement. Before he could utter the next word, Pompe had hit him with his whip. The others immediately joined in a murderous assault on the lone young Jew. A few seconds later his glasses flew off his nose onto the ground where Pompe stomped on them. I will never forget the sound the breakage produced. Bornstein, now blinded, crouched on the floor trying to protect his face with his arms – but to no avail. The flailing and whipping rained down on him until his clothes were beaten off him. There was blood everywhere. His eyes were gone as he lay on his back with these men kicking his body. Pompe seemed out of his mind in his fury. Hopping around on his one good leg in order to maintain balance, he sent his wooden booted leg again and again into near dead Bornstein's body. I stood there completely transfixed, not knowing what to do. At last the beatings stopped. Prisoners were called in who carried poor Bornstein to the coal chute under the wash barrack. There they dumped him into the blackness of the cellar.

Leaving the refectory, Mr. Gebuehrer lay his hand on my head. I was so scared; I think I wept. "Come on," he said to me. On arrival in his little room, he kicked open the box under the table and said, "*Mein Kleiner*, you must forget what you saw. Have something to eat."

That night we heard some ghastly, otherworldly howling coming from the wash barrack direction. The terrifying noise did not resemble human sounds. I lay on my bunk and shivered. It must have been toward morning that the sounds subsided and I fell asleep. Bornstein had died.

Naturally I was not the only one who was aware of what had happened the previous day. After the usual morning roll call during which, to everyone's joy, no one was selected for death, I returned to my room. Several men sat there and discussed the sad event. One of them expressed wonderment that no miracle had occurred to save the young man. "Surely, *HaShem* ("the name," circumlocution for the biblical name of God) must have seen and heard what was happening,"

## *In the midst of hell: Brande*

he advanced. Another man chimed in, saying, "Of course, he did. And we can be sure that Bornstein is now safe and in good hands." Yet another fellow began laughing. "So where do you think the poor guy is right now?" The answer came quickly: "Of course, in heaven. Where else?" Then there was silence.

I did not know what to think. I was terrified. My only hope for me was Mr. Gebuehrer's favorable attitude toward me. But there were also questions. How and how long will I survive this hell? Who will come to get me out of here? I am so terribly alone here. Oh, if only Tati and Mutti were here to help me, to console me. A wild mishmash of thoughts washing over the brain of a sixteen-year-old. The only solace I could think of instinctively was Lydia's little pendant. And so I clutched it in my sweaty hand. My chest felt like exploding with emptiness.

Despite my relative safety in Brande, even I had to dodge danger daily. Pompe would appear within the camp quite often and unannounced. For instance, at any moment roll call would be announced, but not the ordinary one. This special roll call was the infamous *Staubappel* or "dust roll call." Having been given notice an hour before, we had to assemble with our two blankets (which had been vigorously shaken, to extract the dust out of them, and neatly folded) held at arm length in front of us. Pompe would then pass by and with his whip test the blankets for their dust content. He would have any guilty person, with dusty blankets, step forward and be publicly beaten by the *Kapos*. In view of the fact that it was virtually impossible to shake out the dust even by means of the most vigorous shaking of the blankets, it was a sure thing that on these occasions there would be some men who would be thrashed.

The winters in central Europe in those years were severe with much snow and ice. In the barracks we shivered both day and night because the rations of wood for the wood stoves were inadequate. But there was one place within the camp that was always comfortably warm: the cobblers' shop. Fortunate were the shoemakers in that shop, because they were always well supplied with wood. Their job was producing and repairing the boots for the German guard personnel and for the *Kapos*. Because the melting and applying of liquid waxes were part of the production process of the boots, the wood stoves in their shop had always to be properly fired. On one occasion when it was especially cold, I entered the shoemakers' shop, stationed myself close to one of their ovens, and rubbed my hands against each other to warm up. It so happened that a few moments later Pompe walked into the shop for a boot fitting. Seeing me there he gruffly asked, "And what are you doing here? Have you suddenly become a cobbler?" I was petrified. "No sir," I answered, "I have come here to warm my hands." Breaking out into a demonic laughter, he responded with, "Well then, let me help you warm another part of your body." At his bidding three *Kapos* arrived in an instant. Having me bend over one of the low stools on which the cobblers sat, one *Kapo* put my head between his knees, the other two each grabbed one of my feet, and Pompe with his whip laid it into me. I cannot describe the pain of the lashing I received. It felt as if someone were cutting right into my flesh. After a few of the hits I passed out. When I came to I found myself on my bunk, so sore that I could hardly move. But that was not all. After I had sufficiently recovered to drag myself from the bunk, I was assigned to a work detail that cleaned the camp latrine. The punishment lasted one week. It consisted of ladling out the excrement from the latrine ditch using large ladles attached to long wooden handles. The excrement was dumped into a wooden cart which was then carted into the woods and dumped into a hole, not unlike the procedure we had followed with Pompe's victims of the wash barrack killings. Even the might of Mr. Gebuehrer was not able to help me. This punishment was executed on the direct order of Pompe.

There was one more incident that terribly upset me. One early morning, it must have been around five, on my way to Mr. Gebuehrer's little room, I heard a conversation taking place at one corner of the camp fences. Sneaking up closer under the cover of darkness very

## In the midst of hell: Brande

carefully so that I would not be detected, I saw an elderly Jewish inmate standing by the fence, trying to fasten his blanket to the barbed wire. I knew immediately what he was trying to do. The old man had in all probability wet the blanket during the night and was now trying to get it dried and aired out. Wetting one's blanket with urine or by means of masturbation was strictly forbidden. Pompe himself would every so often burst into a barrack in the middle of the night for an inspection. Woe to the prisoner whose blanket was found moist, let alone wet. Beatings would be administered right then and there. Obviously the old man at the fence was trying to make sure that such a fate was not awaiting him. Here then was the conversation I overheard:

"You, over there, you filthy Jew swine, what do you think you are doing?"

The old man shivered and trembled. "I am hanging up my blanket to dry," he uttered in Yiddish.

The guard, pointing his rifle at the man: "Just you go ahead now. Hang it up!" With these words said, he fired and the old man fell to the ground.

That morning at roll call, with the dead body of the old man lying on the ground in the middle of the *Appelplatz*, Pompe gave a speech. "This is what happens to prisoners who are stupid enough to attempt fleeing. Don't you make the same mistake," he warned us, "or you will end up like him." Kicking the dead man's body, he turned around and walked out of the camp.

This then was the convalescence camp Brande. Despite my privileged status I was pleased when, shortly after this incident, during a roll call, the infamous SS officer called the *soykher* selected me with a number of other prisoners for transfer to another camp.

CHAPTER 8
# From Brande to Klettendorf

And so I was finally transferred from Brande. I was glad to leave that hell, but as always in such a transfer, I feared what the future was holding in store for me. In Brande I profited from the protecting relationship with Mr. Gebuehrer and as a result had no lack of food. Agreed that it was only bread that was available to me, still this meant having an intake of a basic staple necessary for survival. A number of young people who shared the Brande experience with me were murdered, as reported earlier, but many also died because of insufficient nourishment.

The sequel to Brande consisted of five forced labor and concentration camps: Gräditz, Nimptsch, Klettendorf, Schmiedeberg and Waldenburg/Gross-Rosen.

The Holocaust-related literature numbers by now thousands of articles and books. This is why there is no point replicating all this misery here. The theme is always the same; the variations differ. What I will attempt to do is to limit my reporting to a few salient happenings from this three-year-long "valley of the shadow of death" (Psalm 23). That suffices.

For one reason or another – I cannot explain it – much of the Gräditz experience is lost to me. What I do remember is that the camp of Gräditz lay more or less adjacent to an underground German air force installation in which we were put to work to move heavy furniture. I remember, for instance, the huge glass screen with maps and flashing arrows and colored dots and circles. Thinking about these displays in retrospect, I venture to guess that these screens were used to monitor the constant movement of aircraft and units of the German fleet. What stands out from the Gräditz experience was our ability to scrounge through the trash containers that were stationed along the streets within the base. I remember the bits of food, especially chunks of bread, often turned green with mold, plucked from an array of other trash deposited there and ravenously devoured by us. Hard and even impossible to understand to this very day is that this rotting food stuff ingested by me did not cause either immediate or lasting damage to my body. Of course, we all suffered from diarrhea on and off and sadly, for some of us this spelled death. I, luckily, was spared from lasting degenerative effects. In retrospect, I get the impression that the Gräditz camp was relatively mild in its treatment of the prisoners.

Sometimes I wonder whether my poor recollection of life in the Gräditz camp is a matter of unconscious selective amnesia, my brain protecting me from remembering something terrible that I may have witnessed there. I do not know. It might just be better this way.

\* \* \* \* \* \* \* \* \* \* \* \* \*

Quite often I am asked how it was that I survived. The answer I give is, "I was lucky, when others were not." Especially Christians in my audience are shocked by this answer, because, in their opinion, I should know that it was God and/or God's angels who protected me. "God had other plans for you," I hear them say. I cannot subscribe to their view of attributing my survival to God's protection. I do not and wish not to see me singled out in some way by God from the rest of world Jewry, of whom one-third perished by Hitler and his henchmen during the Holocaust. How could God make me survive while one and a half million innocent children went to their death without God intervening on their behalf? Does not acceptance of such thoughts border on obscenity? Or is it that we simply do not understand God's ways – a thought often expressed in the Bible? As his creatures and as Jews, are we not to be thankful to God for all that comes into our lives, both good and bad?

Sorry, but I cannot accept this. This smacks too much of simplistic Calvinism.

\* \* \* \* \* \* \* \* \* \* \* \* \*

Nimptsch, the next camp, remains very clear in my memory. It was a very small camp, one oriented exclusively to the performance of a single task. The project to be executed was the shipping of thousands of wooden cases, each containing two fifty-kilogram bombs. The wooden containers were housed in an enormous building, several stories high, in the midst of which was an open shaft. At its highest point, suspended from the roof over the gaping shaft, was an electric winch equipped with an operator's seat. It was I who was designated to sit in this contraption hanging above the open shaft and to operate the winch that lifted the bomb cases from the edge of the shaft on the various floors and lowered them to the bottom of the building, from where prisoner teams loaded them on trucks. These vehicles, in turn, transported the bomb cases to the train station where other prisoner teams transferred them into the railroad cars. The work was done under the supervision of not only camp guards but also personnel of the German *Luftwaffe* or Air Force.

Nimptsch, as I indicated, housed at the very most two hundred prisoners. The food, as everywhere else, was inadequate while the work of the prisoners was exhausting. I was very fortunate in that sitting in the contraption under the roof and operating its four levers did not require physical strength. What it did demand was utmost concentration and quite a bit of skill so as not to injure my fellow prisoners, let alone German personnel below by letting the crates descend too fast, injuring or even crushing them. The work was demanding also because these were bombs we were handling. I never found out whether they were armed or not, but I do remember Air Force men cautioning me on a number of occasions of the great danger involved in handling the large cases.

Once again I was lucky because sitting up there in the winch basket and merely pushing and pulling levers was easy work. As a result, the depletion of my strength progressed more slowly than that of my comrades below whose work was very hard.

Because the performance of this work was critical to the German war effort and had to proceed on schedule, and also because the work of handling the heavy crates efficiently demanded strength and skill, we were not overly abused by the camp guards. The delimited scope of the operation done by a relatively small work force lent itself to camaraderie among the prisoners. This was perhaps the only camp where two fellow prisoners befriended me. They were Austrian brothers from Vienna. Contrary to the rest of the prisoners who spoke either Polish, Yiddish or both, we spoke German with each other, and that fact alone resulted in a special bond between us. These brothers, both older, taller and more robust than I, became my friends and quasi protectors. And so Nimptsch was one camp in which I did not feel totally alone and abandoned. We knew, of course, that with the emptying of the bomb cases from the huge building, our days in Nimptsch were numbered. Often in our bedtime conversations we speculated when this time would come and what our future would be then. I also remember talking with these fellows about the political situation: when and how would this terrible war, and with it our situation, come to an end? Cut off from the rest of the world, we had no access to the news, and so our conversations remained within the sphere of assumptions, opinions and mostly hope.

And then one day I lowered the last bomb case down to the ground floor. With it the job was completed and the camp of Nimptsch dissolved. The *soykher* arrived punctually and to my great chagrin my Austrian friends and I were separated and transferred.

The next camp was Klettendorf, a rather large camp with several hundred prisoners. When we lined up for roll call after arrival I was pleasantly surprised to see among the *Kapos* an old acquaintance from prewar times, a certain Harry Haubenstock. Here he was, the good looking young man whom both my sister and my cousin had an adolescent crush on, son of a client of my father's, arrayed in riding pants and black boots with a whip in his hand, shouting commands in German. Seeing this prewar acquaintance from the town of Karviná, a neighboring town to Teschen, here in Klettendorf, was a favorable omen. Would he turn out to be my protector as Gebuehrer was in Brande? Would he perhaps invite me to become his *faifus*, a term commonly applied to personal servants of *Kapos* and other privileged people in the concentration camp world? These *faifuses*, who constituted the third tier in the camp hierarchy right under the Kapos, often had *faifuses* themselves. This was the social pecking order in the camps, and while condemned by the ordinary prisoners, the system had the advantage of a sort of trickle-down economy which benefited a good number of people.

While Harry Haubenstock recognized me all right as an old acquaintance, he made no move, to my great disappointment, to help me in any way. He already had a *faifus* in the person of Peter Berger, a fellow from our common prewar geographical area, about two years older than I. Other than being recognized with a few words by Haubenstock as an acquaintance, the development of a relationship between us – that depended entirely on his initiative – did not go anywhere.

Klettendorf for me was an especially difficult camp because of its harsh work conditions. We built a railroad line which involved laying of rails, nailing them to the cross beams, and carrying these assembled and very heavy dual-rail segments to the place where they would be connected to the already existing line. It was backbreaking work, exacerbated by the constant yelling of the *Kapos* to accelerate our output and the lashings we received on our backs. I never once worked in one of Haubenstock's groups, and I also never saw him mistreating a prisoner. For that I am grateful, because after the war it was this same Harry Haubenstock who married my cousin Ilse.

Every so often a person collapsed from exhaustion during the process of carrying the rail modules. This resulted in the stumbling of others, a sort of domino effect that infuriated the guards who then began cursing and indiscriminately whipping the whole group. Even after order was reestablished, that fallen man went missing, which resulted in an uneven distribution of the heavy load which, in turn, led to more accidents of similar kind.

I do not remember any longer in which camp our by now worn and torn clothes were discarded in favor of the blue and white stripe pajama-like concentration camp-type uniforms we were destined to wear for the rest of our imprisonment. This may have taken place in the next camp by the name of Schmiedeberg, but I am not sure. It may have also been here that the transition from slave labor camp to concentration camp took place.

The textile of the new-to-us but already worn uniforms was of a very loose weave. One could literally see through the material. The sum total of our dress from this point on consisted of a pair of pants, a shirt and a jacket. No underwear was to be had at any time. Our heads were covered by a beret made of the same material. We were given a square piece of this same material to serve as socks, which had to be carefully folded and slipped into the shoes, the latter consisting of thick wooden soles with a cloth top, held together with a pair of shoe laces. Folding this square cloth carefully was very important because neglecting to do so could very easily cause chafing of toes and other parts of the foot, eventually developing into open sores. These sores might get infected, and an open infected sore would prevent one from keeping up with the tempo of the rest of the column marching to and from work or, at worst, prevent one altogether from walking. Inability to perform the work in camp or on the construction site would then turn into a death sentence: death within the camp or transport to an extermination camp like Auschwitz.

As time went on, the state of this clothing deteriorated, of course. We worked in it and we slept in it. There was infestation of lice, which burrowed under our skins. The vermin had to be carefully extracted, a ritual we repeated every evening before we crawled into our bunks. The delousing, as we called it, was a procedure crucially important because lice, unless carefully extracted from under the skin without leaving any of its parts in there, represented the danger of infection resulting in inability to work and therefore danger of execution. The delousing process consisted of inspecting one another's bodies for the presence of lice, their careful extraction, and the scraping of louse eggs out of the seams of our uniforms. In certain camps, as for instance in Brande, we experienced infestations by bedbugs as well. Because of their bites, the same cautionary procedures had to be taken to prevent infection.

With difficulties on the eastern front and under constant bombing attacks, Germany's military might was slowly weakening. As the defeats multiplied, the conditions in the concentration camps kept deteriorating. There was less food to be had, and the quality of the only solid food, the bread, went from bad to worse. This deterioration also applied to the physical living conditions in the camps. So for instance, for reasons unknown to us, lack of water occurred now ever more frequently in the wash barracks. Hand in hand with the decreased availability of water – quite often totally empty faucets – went an ever-increasing difficulty of maintaining even minimally one's personal hygiene.

One of the most dreaded moments of camp life was the twice daily roll call which more often than not lasted over an hour. The morning roll calls were especially traumatic in wintertime. While standing at attention and being counted over and over again, the number of prisoners hardly ever tallying because of deaths occurring during the night or the previous day on the construction site, there was the ordeal of having to deal with physical urges. It was inconceivable to ask to be excused for a visit to the latrine. And so, especially elderly people whose muscle control had diminished had no choice but to urinate or, in worse cases, to defecate into their pants. I remember how, when the order finally came to turn right and march, some of these poor folks were immobilized because the trickled down urine had frozen their wooden shoes to the snow or ice below and they were unable to move. Fellow prisoners, noticing their dilemma, would smack their shoes against the frozen ones in an attempt to free them. Most of the time this procedure met with success. But all was not necessarily well even then, because several inches of snow may have attached themselves to one shoe while the other one was clean. And so these folks now limped and often turned their ankles on the march to work. When they fell, which happened quite often, we had no choice but to march right over them, leaving them behind lying in the snow. Then a shot would be heard behind us, and we all knew what that meant. Roll call was dreaded by us all, probably even more so than the excruciating work at the construction sites.

It may have been in Gräditz that the identification of prisoners by number was begun. When for the first time I received the concentration camp uniform which, by the way, was not new but must have been worn by someone before me about whose fate I never speculated, there were two small stripes of cloth with a stamped-on number attached to the jacket on the front left side and on its back between the shoulder blades. The same number was also attached to the back side of the right pant leg at knee height. The number I happened to receive was 64757. From that moment on I lost my proper name. In the eyes of the Nazis I was now nothing more than an object that could be manipulated any way they pleased: a number. Identification by number rather than by name robbed us of our human identity, our personhood. This act, combined with our loss of hair and being forced into identical clothing, transformed us from humans into objects. As we all know, it is easier to dispose of objects than human beings. The Nazi murderers simplified for themselves the task of killing Jews whenever possible. Their meticulous bookkeeping may have also been facilitated by making numbers out of us.

\* \* \* \* \* \* \* \* \* \* \* \* \*

The great Jewish philosopher, theologian and Biblical scholar, Martin Buber, was prophetic with his book *I and Thou*, in which he differentiated the "I – Thou" relationship from the "I – It" one. In the latter, the "It" is defined as an object to be used and even exploited by the "I," the subject, to achieve self-satisfaction. The quintessential realization of the "I – It" relationship took place in Nazi Germany where the Jews were reduced to the "It" status and then easily disposed of as mere objects. Human beings, all "subjects" by definition, were made into "objects" by the Germans. It should be no surprise that Zyklon-B, a powerful insecticide used to eliminate all sorts of vermin, was used in the mass gassing factory at Auschwitz and elsewhere to murder human beings who by the Nazis were considered nothing more than vermin, cockroaches.

By transforming us, dignified human beings, into ugly, filthy, repulsive-looking human skeletons, we became objects to be gotten rid of. Looking at us must have conjured up feelings of disgust in those who saw us. Because of intense continuous hate education against the Jews that Nazi Germany engaged in, it did not occur to the men and women who had imbibed the demonization of the Jews over a number of years that it was they, passive onlookers and often perpetrators, who were the real cause for our deterioration into subhumanity. They were the "I's" and we, who were formerly "I's," too, had become the "Its," dangerous and disgusting objects, the scum of humanity, fit for elimination. We had become *Untermenschen*, subhumans, with whom all social intercourse had to be prevented in order to prevent contamination and spreading the Jew-disease. If the long hate-and-demonizing education against the Jews succeeded so well, it was because it fell on fertile ground prepared during the prior nineteen centuries by the religion-based antisemitic teachings of the Christian churches.

In Buber's view the Bible mandates for us humans the "I – Thou" relationship. This means that in our dealings with each other, in human-to-human intercourse, it must always be a "subject" addressing another "subject" or an "I" addressing another "I." This mandate is predicated on God's alleged relationship to us humans. God, according to Buber, never deals with us as "subject to object." God deals with us as autonomous "subjects" or "I's."

I am not so sure that after the Holocaust Buber would have continued to justify the "I – Thou" relationship among human beings by invoking the God – Israel relationship found in the Bible. As I see God's relationship to humans and more particularly to the Jews during the Holocaust, it is complete abandonment.

The alternative to God's abandonment can also simply be the non-existence of God altogether. In that case Buber's justification of "I – Thou" on the basis of God's relationship to humanity is a moot issue. To me, in any case, the necessity of "I – Thou" is much more a matter of common sense than some supreme wisdom communicated to us from above. It is worth observing in this connection that Rabbi Hillel (1st century B.C.), in the Talmudic tractate *Avot*, did not invoke God as his source when he taught, "What is hateful to you, do not do unto your neighbor." Humanity must respect other's humanity. Human dignity respects the other's human dignity. It is as simple as that.

CHAPTER 9
# Schmiedeberg, Waldenburg and liberation

In Schmiedeberg there awaited me an important, unexpected and unpleasant surprise. Who of all people was there at our first roll call if not my old acquaintance from Brande, *Wachthabender* (officer of the guard) Pompe? When he mustered the newly arrived prisoners from Klettendorf he recognized me, and it was not long after that the Jewish camp-eldest called me to the office to inform me that from the next day on I would be detailed to the personal service of Pompe.

Early the following morning I appeared at Pompe's door outside the camp periphery in one of the barracks assigned to the guards and reported for duty. The little room housed a simple metal bed, a table and two chairs, and a cupboard. I also remember a couple of large ashtrays on that table filled with cigarette butts. Judging from the amount of these, it was clear to me that Pompe was a chain smoker. I thought that his cadaver-like ashen face may have derived from the overuse of tobacco.

My duty, he informed me, was shining his boots, sweeping and dusting his room, cleaning any dishes that I might find there including the ashtrays, and making his bed. All this had to be performed prior to the roll call at which I, just like all the other prisoners, had to appear.

The prisoner camp in Schmiedeberg was located in proximity of the construction site or *Baustelle*. We were involved in building steel reinforced concrete buildings and bunkers. The steel reinforcements consisted of rebars of various diameter, bent into various shapes which, in combination with certain other wire forms, were wired together by hand to form three-dimensional skeletal bodies. These were lowered in between wooden retaining walls and fastened there. Then concrete was poured into the void formed by the wooden retaining plates, and thus a concrete wall came into being. The procedure was pretty much the same as used today for pouring foundations or walls for buildings, with the difference that today, most of the time, the retaining walls are metallic. Once the concrete had set, we removed the wooden forms and the concrete wall was free-standing.

The prisoners were involved in all stages of this construction. It was a scary experience to work deep down in these wooden shafts and to hear the concrete being poured almost next to one. The proximity of the quickly rising concrete often necessitated a very fast exit by climbing up rapidly because otherwise one might get caught in the swelling grey mass of the mixture of cement, gravel and water and be entombed by it. And so at the first noise of the pouring we scrambled out from below as fast as we could. It happened twice that a prisoner was caught down there in the grey mass and was buried alive.

The factory which we were in the process of expanding was located within a mountain. A railroad and an automobile/truck road led into the mountain through an entrance gate, and there was constant traffic flowing into and emerging from the tunnel. Rumor had it that inside the mountain there was a production facility for V-2 rockets, those unguided ram-jet missiles with which the Nazis bombarded England. Retired professor Hermann Weiss of the University of Michigan, a native of Schmiedeberg, contacted me several years ago to gain information concerning my experience as a prisoner in the Schmiedeberg slave labor camp. In one of his communications he informed me that

## Schmiedeberg, Waldenburg and liberation

according to his research, the factory produced heavy artillery munition and airplane wing tanks rather than V-2's. What I saw entering and exiting the tunnel gate were stacked two-to-three-meter long metal half shell-like forms which, when put together, would have formed a large projectile-type object.

Not far from the entrance to the tunnel there was a roofed shed under which the rebars were bent into various configurations by an electrically operated machine. Prisoners carried straight rebars from where they lay stacked to this machine and then fed them individually into it. A young Jewish prisoner operated the machine. This required a certain skill, but no expending of physical strength. The machine was dangerous to operate because of its long and heavy rotating steel arm that extended beyond the rectangular top of the machine. By placing the bars between a stationary heavy steel peg and one such peg on the rotating arm, the heavy steel bars were bent into shape. If not paid proper attention, that arm could catch the operator's left thigh and smash it.

And this is unfortunately what happened one day to the young man operating the machine. His left foot, operating the direction of rotation of the machine arm by means of a foot pedal, was forcibly pressed against that pedal in the "go" position because his thigh above had been caught and squeezed by the rotating arm against the flat top of the machine. After a few heartrending screams that called our attention to the boy's dilemma, we rushed over and tried to extricate him. His upper body had by then collapsed over the machine, whose motor was still running despite the jammed position of the heavy metal arm. With his thigh firmly wedged between the machine's top and the rotational arm, we tried to reverse the rotation of the metal arm, but to no avail. By the time the electricians and mechanics arrived, the young fellow seemed lifeless. When finally freed, they carried his limp body to a truck and drove off.

The construction foreman acted quickly. "You see what happened to this poor guy," he said to me. "Be more careful when you operate the machine!" With these words I was promoted to my next job behind the killer machine that had a few minutes earlier claimed its victim.

Naturally, the danger of operating this machine intimidated me. But seeing death all around me and having gotten used to it by now, this particular incident did not make much of an impact on me. The time must have been winter 1944, and I had by then spent almost three years in these hellish camps, which experiences had blunted my sensitivities. At this point I saw only the advantage of doing work that would not be physically demanding. The human instinct of self-preservation kicked in, as it were, and so I stepped into the shoes of my predecessor who by now had probably died or was murdered, and began bending rebars.

I watched that long rotating arm very carefully, and I actually enjoyed the new job. Coupled with some of the leftovers I was able to scrounge up at my job with Pompe, I felt that I was at least slowing the physical and mental deterioration that advanced in all of us inexorably. Then an interesting incident occurred that is worth repeating here because it illustrates how we Jews were stereotyped by the Germans. One day the construction site foreman called me to his office. As I walked behind him at a rather fast clip through the mud and the numerous puddles of the construction site, the cloth tops of my wooden shoes became totally soaked. I could just feel my feet getting wetter and wetter. Not so his, of course. The foreman wore a pair of knee-high black rubber boots. Impermeable as these were, he slushed through all this mess at a rapid pace without paying the least attention to the wet dirt and the water puddles. "If only I had a set of such rubber boots!" I said to myself. Many a night, after returning to the camp soaked, I dreamed of rubber boots. To this day, as I slip into my own rubber boots before going to work in my garden, I feel truly privileged to own such a treasure. Rare are the times when donning the boots in the garage that I do not remember how much I coveted this man's boots. As I write this I realize

## Schmiedeberg, Waldenburg and liberation

that to the reader all this must sound bizarre and even silly. Dreaming, of all things, about rubber boots?

Arriving at the foreman's shed, I saw a number of blueprints spread over a large table, showing the different shapes into which we were bending the rebars. Pointing his finger to one of the shapes I was presently bending, he said to me in German, "You see, young fellow, that this dimension has to be changed." I took a good look at the changed blueprint and noticed that when adding up a certain number of dimensions, their total did not correspond to the number of the total indicated on the blueprint. I pointed out the discrepancy to the foreman because I realized that given the dimensions indicated, I would not be able to produce the desired product. Naturally, I spoke to him in my native German language. When I had made my argument, he shook his head in disbelief. "You are not a Jew, young fellow. How is it that you are here?" "Of course I am a Jew," I responded. "It is precisely because I am a Jew that I am here." The foreman kept on shaking his head. "But Jews don't speak German," he countered. "All this just doesn't make sense!" With these words he walked to a filing cabinet, opened it, removed his lunch box and gave me one of the sandwiches he had brought from home. Without saying a word he handed me the bread and said, "You better eat this here."

This is one of only two incidents during my three-year long captivity in which I experienced a German showing compassion for a Jew. The incident, while isolated, buoyed up my spirit. It occurred at a time when I desperately needed this kind of mental uplift because of what had happened a few days before.

With a transport of Jewish prisoners that arrived a few days earlier came a young fellow approximately my age who recognized me. This was Janek, a boy whom I briefly befriended in Brande. Janek looked relatively good. He was the *faifus* of a *Kapo* by the name of Kaminsky, and they had passed together through a number of camps. Janek, recognizing me, walked up to me and in a nasty tone remarked,

"So also you have by now become an *uchol*, Walter!" The words cut straight into my heart. The term *uchol* was the equivalent of the better known word *Muselmann* used to describe those zombie-like concentration camp prisoners with large protruding eyes devoid of all expression, skeletal bodies, and distended bellies. There were no mirrors in the camps, and so the only chance we could see ourselves was in water puddles on the ground or under certain conditions in the windows of our barrack. The use of *uchol* generally applied to prisoners whose number was soon to be up. Death would be imminent. I cannot describe how hurt I was by Janek's thoughtless remark. Surprisingly, it was a German foreman's words a few days later, and that little sandwich he gave me, that mitigated the spirit-demolishing influence my fellow prisoner Janek's cruel words wrought upon my self-esteem. I never spoke with him again.

My privileged position with Pompe came to a halt shortly after. Right after one of his temporary departures for a few days of vacation with his family, I cleaned up his room spic and span, making it ready for his return to the camp. He arrived a few days later and soon after had me report to duty. What I saw as I entered his small room made me cringe for fear: the large ashtrays were filled with cigarette butts; the bed which I had carefully made was in total disarray; the floor was dirty, and under the table lay an empty bottle of wine. I did not have to wait long for Pompe's explosion. Pointing to the bedstead and the ashtray, he yelled at me, "So this is how you do your duty, you filthy Jew boy? So this is how you reward my generosity?" I saw his cadaver-like face turn greenish as he screamed and then kicked me in the belly. As I tumbled into the opposite wall, he came over to me and slapped me in the face over and over again, finally pushing me out of the door. That was the end of my privileged status with *Wachthabender* Pompe in Schmiedeberg.

The camp-eldest to whom I related this incident called me to his office several days later and told me that one of the guards who heard

## Schmiedeberg, Waldenburg and liberation

the ruckus in Pompe's room explained to him what had happened. It seems that Pompe's deputy used the opportunity of his boss's absence to invite a prostitute to spend the evening. They used Pompe's quarters for their drunken sexual carousing, which caused the disorder I encountered when called in. Pompe was of course furious about this insubordination and spewed out his anger against me. And so I had no choice but to lick my wounds and be silent about this whole matter.

It wasn't long before the *soykher* appeared and there was a "selection." My next and last concentration camp was to be Waldenburg, a sub-camp of the infamous Gross-Rosen concentration camp, south of the city of Breslau. The camp was an hour's march from the construction site, located next to a huge industrial complex of the I.G. Farbenindustrie, a company comparable to DuPont or General Motors. Our job was to prepare an area adjacent to the factory for expansion. The topography of that piece of land was several feet higher than desired and consisted of bedrock that had to be blasted and then removed with monster backhoes, loaders and trucks. Our job was to drill holes into the rock surface six to eight inches deep. The German crews would then pack these holes with dynamite, and after evacuating all German workers and prisoners, blast the rock, exposing a new layer which would be treated in similar manner.

The winter of 1944-45 was bitter cold. All the winters in Central Europe were then very severe and the snowfalls significant. I mentioned elsewhere the loosely woven articles of clothing we wore. The shirt and jacket were no match for the cold wind that blew right through them. And there was an additional misery to be dealt with: the tools used for drilling the shallow holes were roughly six to seven-foot long iron bars, tipped with some specially hardened steel. Each hole was drilled by two prisoners facing one another holding between them the long iron rod which had to be lifted about a foot high and then dropped, lifted again, turned a bit and dropped again. Eventually this repetitive process produced a hole for blasting. The steel we held in our hands was naturally ice cold, and holding onto it with bare hands would have meant getting the skin of our hands frozen to it. Trying to let loose of the iron bar under such circumstances would have caused severe tearing of the skin and probable infection. But we were not given gloves for this work! And so we ripped pieces of material from the bottom of our shirts to provide us with just enough material to interpose it between steel and hands. Naturally, this procedure robbed us of a precious piece of cloth under our pants and so further aggravated our exposure to the icy cold weather conditions.

Marching to and from the construction site was pure hell. Snow and ice fastened themselves to the wooden soles of our shoes. Then one side gave way and fell off and so we limped through the snow, always driven on by screamed insults and blows by the guards' rifle butts and the *Kapos*' whips. People stumbled and fell, accidentally or because of sheer exhaustion, only to be walked over and left behind. The sound of a shot behind us spelled out their end.

The roll calls, those hours of pure torture in the morning and evening, increased in length because the number of prisoners constantly changed. The actual number of prisoners lined up for counting hardly ever agreed with their theoretical number on the lists. Every morning some prisoners were found dead, some in their bunks, some electrocuted on the lower inner fence. The latter were suicides committed by those unfortunate ones who could no longer bear living under these hellish circumstances. Every day some of my fellow prisoners expired either at the construction site from exhaustion, or were shot for pleasure or some trumped-up reason. Some among us collapsed during the return march to camp.

That I survived with my life I owe to a couple of Dutch doctors who ran the camp hospital consisting of one room partitioned into a sort of reception and examination area, and a cubicle with three-story high bunk beds.

It happened during an early march to the construction site through

## Schmiedeberg, Waldenburg and liberation

one of the streets of the town of Waldenburg. Out of the shadow from behind a church building there suddenly appeared a figure who threw a little package into the ranks of the prisoners. I happened to catch it. Shots rang out, and I tried hard to defend it against a number of hands attempting to wrest it from me. The packaged contained two thin slices of buttered dark bread, and I barely succeeded in getting a chunk of this treasure into my mouth. We were all so terribly hungry. Food was our main preoccupation throughout the day.

I remember listening to my fellow prisoners tell stories of birthday celebrations and bar mitzvahs, holidays and weddings. The description of food was always at the center of these accounts. When I recall these occasions in retrospect, I am inclined to guess that many of these stories were vastly exaggerated. Almost certainly some of these accounts were feverish chimeras of starved men who dreamed about the past even though that past in reality may have been much less attractive than how it was described. In any case, it was food that was on our minds in day and night dreams.

After the war, when German documentation about conditions in concentration camps became available, it was learned that fourteen ounces of bread was the government-assigned ration for a prisoner. Because prisoners were entrusted with the cutting and distributing eight portions from a round bread, and with favoritism of the bread cutters toward their friends, many of the portions some of us received ended up much smaller than that. A less favored fellow prisoner could easily have ended up with ten ounces only. The daily bread portion being the key to survival, it was this bread, the only solid foodstuff we received, on which most of our conversations focused. Not just the necessary quantity of bread was discussed in detail, but conversations turned ad infinitum on the wisest manner in which this piece of bread should be eaten. Some suggested eating the whole portion in one sitting right after receiving it; others counseled that one eat half of it upon reception, and the other half in the morning before setting out to work; still others advised crumbling up the bread and eating little chunks of it all day long, keeping one's juices flowing, as it were. The half-and-half suggestion, while being the most logical one, was also the most risky one, because of the danger of theft during the night. We all listened to these "bread philosophers" carefully, weighing the relative advantages and disadvantages of the proposed methods of eating the bread. After carefully weighing the various possible approaches, I decided to eat the whole ration in one great and satisfying eating orgy when it was handed out in the evening.

Back to that sandwich thrown into our ranks. That little piece of bread tasted heavenly. We marched on and drilled those holes into bedrock, business as usual. After the evening rituals of eating and delousing ourselves, I took off my shoes before crawling onto my bunk. But at that point I had a surprise coming, because on the outer edge of my right shoe I noticed a ripped hole. Not impressed by this discovery, I continued to undo the rag that served me as a sock. Rather than easily coming loose, it stuck to my foot as if glued on. Tugging on it, I felt a slight hurt in the area, but succeeded in getting the foot bare. At this point a new surprise: a flesh wound in my right foot. Amazingly – something I do not understand to this day, by the way – there was hardly any blood. Just a sticky sort of clear, pinkish fluid.

None of this seemed to perturb me. I lay down on my bunk and fell sound asleep. In retrospect all this suggests to me now how damaged my reasoning capacity had become. None of us thought clearly any longer at this point of our existence. The information processing capacity of our brains had become severely impaired.

The next two or three days went by without any new developments – something difficult for me to understand today. By the fourth day, difficulties set in. I noticed a significant swelling of the foot. There was oozing from the wound and there was discoloring of the surrounding skin. Another couple of days later I could hardly squeeze my foot into the shoe, and walking became very painful. At this point I saw it

## Schmiedeberg, Waldenburg and liberation

necessary to visit the camp physicians in their mini-hospital. When they saw my foot they were visibly disturbed. "Why didn't you come to see us before?" I shrugged my shoulders. And so these two good men went to work on my foot, cleansing the wound with alcohol that sent me into a howl, and with a scalpel cutting off some flesh surrounding the wound. They bandaged me up, gave me aspirin, and insisted that I stay at the hospital. All this leaves us with the question of how this wound in my foot happened to begin with. I mentioned earlier that shots rang out at the moment the bread package was thrown into our ranks. It must have been a stray or ricocheting bullet that hit my right foot. That's the only explanation I can offer. I only hope that the good person who tried to help us with the bread escaped alive, because the bullets were certainly meant for her.

Staying at the camp hospital was a risky affair because of regular controls by the SS personnel who regularly dropped in on the premises. If on one of these triaging visits the Germans found someone who in their opinion was beyond healing, that person was sent to the main camp of Gross-Rosen where they disposed of him at the infamous shooting wall. Gross-Rosen's crematory took care of the rest. To prevent such a thing from happening to me, these two physicians hid me under one of the empty lower bunks by arranging the low tier in such a way that its blankets hung down to the floor on all four sides. Hidden by these blankets, I lay on the floor. Only today can I appreciate the personal risk they took upon themselves by hiding me there. Naturally I have no idea how the count of the prisoners was finagled so as to cover my absence from the work force.

From these harrowing days under the bunk I remember one incident in particular. When on one occasion the blanket curtain was raised by someone to push a bowl of soup toward me, I peeked out from my hiding place. At a distance of perhaps five feet I saw a foot with five black toes and a hand holding a pair of kitchen pliers snapping off those gangrened toes. Not in the least perturbed by the sight,

I hastily drew the bowl of soup toward me and heartily drank the wonderful warm liquid.

A parenthesis might be in place at this point. I am afraid that this lack of sensitivity toward another person's suffering, induced in me probably by necessity as a defensive mechanism against the constant brutality and cruelty to which I was exposed for almost three years, remained with me to some extent. I suffer from guilt feelings as I compare my relative coldness to other folks' signs of emotion. This is not to say that I feel no empathy with those who suffer! It means that the motor that drives my empathy is grounded in intellectual and ethical cognition of what I witness, rather than in something that springs spontaneously from somewhere deep in my emotional disposition. While I know that others would dispute this self-evaluation, I really carry this guilt feeling of insufficient emotion as a burden through life. The only mitigating factor concerning these guilt feelings is my recognition that, should my self-analysis be correct, the failing is not of my own doing. It is yet another unfortunate aftereffect of the curse of Hitler's terror regime that has survived long after Hitler's physical demise.

And so it was the two Dutch Jewish doctors who saved my life. My wound started healing, and perhaps one week or so after my hospitalization I was back among the prisoner workforce.

On May 8, 1945, early in the morning, we stood in our usual formation to be counted. This time, however, the ritual did not take place as usual. I remember looking up at the watchtowers where normally SS men could be seen behind their machine guns trained on us. This morning the towers were unmanned. But the famous Passover question—"Why is this night different from all other nights?"—did not occur to us because our mental processes, which by now had become significantly impaired from starvation of the brain by undernourishment and physical and mental abuse, no longer functioned properly. And so we just stood there like a bunch of cattle, immobile and

## Schmiedeberg, Waldenburg and liberation

passive. Then the triple gates flew open and the *Waffen SS* commander walked in rather leisurely toward the waiting camp-eldest, a German felon, and the *Kapos* that surrounded him. Words were exchanged, after which the SS officer walked out of the camp. Turning left after passing through the gates, he unfastened a large key ring from his belt and threw it over the triple fence into the interior of the camp. As I remember, there was no visible reaction by anyone. We just stood there in formation, waiting.

For several weeks we had been hearing artillery thunder without knowing what it meant. In my recollection this was never questioned in our sparse conversations. By then Germany's victory and our doom were matters taken for granted. No one, absolutely no one, counted on a reversal of the political situation. Nor did anyone mention God and the possibility of a miraculous liberation from the clutches of the Nazis. Frankly, I don't remember that we thought about anything but nagging hunger and our never ending hope for more food.

The rumbling motor noise we now heard approaching and ever increasing in intensity was quite different from the rumbling artillery sounds we had gotten used to. And then we saw its source: a single Soviet tank appearing around the corner of the camp. The tank drove straight into one side of the peripheral triple fence, smashing it, and then rolled on. I remember the soldier standing in the tank turret. He did not wave. He just stood there. Nothing else. Then the tank was gone from sight. One side of the camp fence was now lying smashed on the ground and barely visible. We were free!

"Revenge! We can still catch him! The SS camp commander can't have gotten away very far!" One would expect that such were our first thoughts at liberation. Far from it! We continued standing there for quite a while before it dawned on us that now finally our ordeal had come to an end and that we were actually free.

What then were our first thoughts at this exhilarating moment? First of all, this critical moment did not come across to us as exhilarating. Our brains at this point were dulled and not properly functioning. Second, it was our empty stomachs that called the first signal: food!

I remember the fellow standing next to me, an Austrian man, older than I, turning to me and saying, "Let's go organize something to eat!" With these words he and I set out for the town of Waldenburg through which we had been marching twice a day. The city was now totally deserted: not a single soul to be seen anywhere. We spotted a military truck parked in one of the streets and climbed up to investigate its contents. It was packed full with camouflage-painted food ration cans, and we pried one can open with the help of a screwdriver. What met our eyes was a white fatty substance. Dipping our fingers into the white stuff that smelled good and tasting it, we found it was pork fat. Digging deeper into the can, we found to our delight chunks of pork. And so our eating orgy began right then and there. We feverishly opened can after can and gorged ourselves. My Austrian friend then slit open one of numerous white sacks. Its contents provided our dessert. Its yield was granulated sugar spilling into the truck bed. Now on all fours, we shoveled the sugar into our mouths. Starved animals that we were, we had come onto an indescribably rich cache of food.

From here on, however, I remember nothing because I passed out.

Awaking, I found myself in a bed between two white sheets. A cuckoo clock on the opposite wall announced the hour, which I no longer remember. In an iron bed a few feet away I saw my Austrian friend fast asleep. Then the door opened and a little old woman clad in black walked in. When she noticed that I was awake, she came over and sat down next to me on the bed. "Now it is all over," she said. "We have lost the war and you are free."

Despite hearing the good news from her, I still felt no particular excitement or elation. My brain still was not properly functioning. Exhausted, I fell back asleep.

## Schmiedeberg, Waldenburg and liberation

Eventually we came out of our twilight zone. Eating remained our first priority for several days. The old woman did her best preparing large pots of potato and pea soup for us. She told us that she had seen our foray into the German rations in the truck below her windows and how we both had fainted. A neighbor helped her drag us to her apartment and put us to bed. According to her we remained unconscious for some thirty-six hours.

Once back on our feet we searched neighboring basements in houses devoid of their earlier residents, who must have fled. No one being there to interfere with our activity, suitcases and boxes were opened by us leisurely in search of suitable clothing. It seemed essential to us to get rid of the miserable concentration camp garb as soon as possible, and eventually we hit pay dirt. As we rummaged around in one particular basement and changed clothes, we heard footsteps above that made us pause in our pillaging expedition. Climbing up the stairs to investigate, we encountered an old wrinkled and disheveled woman who made us feel very uncomfortable with her grimacing and animal-like hissing sounds. We followed her to an apartment and to its bedroom with three beds. It was a shocking sight: a German army officer and his wife lying next to each other, he in full regalia and she fully dressed, and a pretty young child in each of the smaller beds, all with a bullet hole in their heads and bloodstains on the pillows. Clearly the father had shot his family and then committed suicide. The sight was so gruesome that we ran head over heels out of that apartment to the grizzly sounds of the old witch-like woman's snickering.

Newly clothed, we returned to, of all places, the camp. What else could we have done after all? Freedom demands making decisions, but that is precisely something which we, after several years in the camps, were no longer capable of doing.

In his book *Survival in Auschwitz*, Primo Levi describes their transport's arrival in Auschwitz from Italy. It was deep winter, and the prisoners had been deprived of food and water for several days. When finally driven into the barracks, Levi saw an icicle suspended from the roof outside the window. He only had to open that window and break off the icicle to quench his terrible thirst. And so he attempted to do just that. But as he was about to break off the icicle, the sharp grip on his arm by a German guard prevented him from doing so. Knowing only a handful of German words, he asked the guard, *"Warum?"* "Why?" – to which the guard grimly responded with, *"Hier gibt es kein 'warum'!"* "Here 'why' does not exist."

In the concentration camp world there was no room for questions. In this underworld one's only choice was listening carefully to the commands given by the guards or *Kapos* and obeying. Only the most courageous among us made decisions: some to attempt escape, some to revolt, and some to kill themselves. Most of the decision makers died in the process of carrying out their resolve. Most of us prisoners were not so courageous as to invite premature death upon ourselves. Death would come sooner or later anyway! Why hasten it? Resistance to the Germans was futile. And there was also the fear that one person's insubordination would easily bring about the death of others. The Germans did not shrink from mass reprisals against their prisoners. Finally, there was also hope. There was hope, even though ever so unrealistic, that Messiah would show up and make an end to the German regime. Many Jewish prisoners placed their hope in the twelfth article of Maimonides' Thirteen Articles of Faith where it is stated, "I believe with perfect faith that Messiah will come. And even though he may tarry, still I hope for his coming." We are told that some Jews marched to the gas chambers of Auschwitz with this confession of faith on their lips. But Messiah did not come, and they perished asphyxiated in those gas chambers by the hundreds of thousands. It was the Allies who put an end to the Holocaust, not Messiah or God.

Having successfully discarded the old camp *shmattes* (rags) and acquired clothes that normal free people wore, we returned to concentration camp Waldenburg. Nothing much had changed during our

## Schmiedeberg, Waldenburg and liberation

absence. Most prisoners still wearing their blue-and-white striped prison uniforms were sitting around small fires, roasting potatoes, beets and perhaps even a piece of meat, relishing their new diet. My Austrian buddy and I joined these shadow-like men. Nothing much was said around the fires. There was mostly silence. Had the will to live disappeared in these people? Or was it an instinctive fear that despite our physical survival, life – as we had known and enjoyed it before the war – had come to an end? Were any of our family members still alive? If so, how will I find them? If not, what am I to do? The future loomed before us as a huge threatening question mark.

The following day women from a neighboring women's concentration camp began appearing among us. They and we were desperately searching for familiar faces. For quite a while in my shyness I did not dare question these women with regard to my mother, sister and cousin. Might one of these women, by some outside chance, have run into one of my relatives somewhere? Screwing up my courage, I finally walked up to a group of three women and blurted out my question: "Did perhaps someone among you, in your camps, meet one or two women by the name of Ziffer?" The answer came quickly from two of them: "Yes, I knew two Ziffer ladies in my last camp." "And where was this? Please tell me!" The response was Langenbielau, a women's camp about thirty kilometers away. "This is where we are coming from."

Without taking leave of any of my fellow prisoners, I rushed back to the city of Waldenburg. My brain now began functioning again. I was terribly agitated. When I saw a German civilian approaching on a bicycle, I barred his way and ordered him off it. The man obeyed immediately, clearly afraid of this horrible apparition that I was then. It took me two days to pedal the distance, and I still remember the night I spent in an open field under the friendly blinking stars. Hope reborn can transform us under the most terrible circumstances. The following afternoon I arrived at Langenbielau camp. In response to my inquiry, I was shown to a barrack full of women who welcomed me in the friendliest of ways. "Yes, this is the barrack where the two Ziffer women and Ilse Borger reside," I was told. "They must surely be out somewhere 'organizing' food. Just sit down, and have something to drink while waiting." The cup of coffee I was served tasted to me like nectar and ambrosia, and I began relaxing a bit despite the excitement that filled my chest. And then it happened: the door opened and barely ten feet from me there walked in my mother, sister and cousin, loaded down with paper sacks, all haggard-looking as can be, with shorn heads, but recognizable. As I sat there transfixed, immobilized by the sight of my family, the three women gave me a friendly nod and walked right by me to the corner of the barrack where they unloaded their goodies. No sign of recognition for me, nothing! Overcoming my temporary paralysis, I walked unsteadily over to them and stutteringly introduced myself. There was stunned silence first, for just one moment. Could this be really happening? Is this reality or a dream? Then a veritable explosion of happiness: laughter and tears, embraces and kisses, a flood of questions. "How terrible you look, Walti! Hell is over now. We'll put some meat on your bones quickly. Are you hungry, Walti?" Words fail me to describe our reunion. This must be lived to be believed.

What lay behind us was pure hell, indeed. Given that horror, it is amazing to me that I emerged from the wholesale destruction of European Jewry relatively unharmed. After my Holocaust-related lectures, I have frequently been asked how in the light of past suffering I succeeded in regaining and maintaining my humanity. There are, sadly, Holocaust survivors who unlike me became permanently depressed and alienated from the new world they encountered after liberation. One Jewish woman once said to me, "Walter, you are the best adjusted Holocaust survivor I ever met, and I have met many of them."

In truth, I have no idea why and how I survived. Suggestions such as "your guardian angels protected you," or "you made it through

## Schmiedeberg, Waldenburg and liberation

because God had a special plan for you" do not make sense to me. I do not believe in angels or a special plan from above that protected me for the simple reason that many more valuable women and men than I, people more worthy of being saved, perished. Those who perished might have made more important contributions to society after the war than I ever did. These "God, angel, and special plan" remarks, while surely well-meant, strike me as downright obscene. This kind of God and heavenly assembly I cannot believe in, much less appreciate.

So let me say again that I have no clue why I survived. But do let me at this point share one of my wife Gail's thoughts, a mere clue to what may have been a contributing factor to my ability to live when so many others died. I have alluded elsewhere to my wonderful relationship with my parents before the war. Not until Gail and I talked about all this extensively was I aware that such a relationship was an extraordinarily privileged one. Not all parents give their children the kind of quality time my father and mother did. Mutti heaped her love upon Edith and me through her daily care for us, her cooking, her oversight of homework, her tender care when we were sick and needed extra attention, her compassion when we hurt, the cuddling we engaged in with her. The list of her loving interactions with us has no end. Tati was the stern, demanding, but equally loving, educator-father. I remember Edith and me sitting at the foot of his bed under the same comforter, listening in rapture to him as he read to us. We were exposed to the finest in world literature on a continuing basis from our childhood on to adolescence through his intelligent choices of books we were urged to read and through the discussions that followed. By age twelve I had read works by Schiller, Goethe, Heine, Shakespeare, Dickens, Molière, Flaubert, Poe, Zola and so on. Our long Sunday walks, hand in hand, with conversation flowing between us, were sources of incredible enrichment. The time Tati spent helping me with building models from construction sets, teaching Edith and me shorthand, explaining to us the workings of chess and checkers with immense patience, the sharing with us the beauty of music – all these, Gail suggested, implanted within me a feeling of security. The unqualified love we received and experienced implanted in us feelings of human dignity and self-reliance. It is likely that possessing such qualities does indeed help a person resist adversity.

My father, now long dead, has been all along my best living teacher. My mother, now long dead, has been my best teacher by example of what it is to lovingly relate to others. And so what I have been over the years after liberation and what I am today I owe to a great extent to these two truly great human beings.

CHAPTER 10
# Difficult return home

The reunion with my mother, sister Edith, and cousin Ilse exceeds description. There are no adequate words to describe our joy at having found one another alive after years of separation and suffering. What happened during the next few days has slipped my memory. All I remember is that somewhat later there appeared in the camp two men who joined us in our effort to return home.

Repatriation was not an easy matter in those days. While the distance between the camp and Teschen was not considerable, we were constantly slowed because bridges across rivers had been blown up by the retreating German army. Every so often a peasant on whose door we knocked asking for food would take us in. From them we received bread and milk as well as a place to rest in the barn. There we would spend the day until evening, when we set out again on our travel homeward. Why travel at night? Because Soviet soldiers roamed the area, and no woman was safe from them. We were repeatedly warned about these men who indiscriminately raped women, including women recently liberated from concentration camps. I remember an inn in which we tried to obtain shelter for the day. The innkeeper showed us to a couple of rooms in which the mattresses were stained with blood. The look the innkeeper gave us in silence told the whole story. We accepted his offer nevertheless, barricaded ourselves in, and spent the day sleeping on the floor.

We must have been on the road close to two weeks, walking and sometimes in the evening hours hitching a ride with a peasant on a horse-drawn carriage. At one point we passed the tent of a refugee aid organization and we were measured and weighed and given an identity paper with our names, vital personal information and concentration camp identity number. This is how I know that at liberation I weighed eighty-seven pounds.

It was a long and arduous journey. We finally arrived in Teschen, walking toward the center of town, all six of us, marching side by side. I no longer remember how I felt. Was the event emotional? I don't remember. What I do remember, however, is a woman running up to my mother and saying rather disappointedly, "So you are back alive, Mrs. Ziffer. Amazing!" The woman was Mrs. Novotný, a Czech woman and wife of our town's pharmacist. A few steps farther into town, another woman recognized my mother. With her the welcoming speech was of a different tone. Excitedly and happily she welcomed us home. "And, Mrs. Ziffer, do you know that your husband arrived here also a few days ago? He lives with your previous housekeeper Malci." The news struck us like a happy bolt of lightning. Our beloved Tati had also survived the deportation – nothing less than a miracle! Our nuclear family would once again be united. Poor cousin Ilse unfortunately could not expect similar good news about her parents. We knew already that both her parents had perished at Auschwitz with all the rest of the deportees from Teschen.

My mother dispatched me to my father as a messenger of our return. Malci Kurjan, our pre-war live-in maid, lived close by, and so I set out to bring my father the good news of our return. My heart probably missed a few beats when I rang the bell and good old Malci, whom my sister and I loved dearly, came to open the door. We warmly embraced, after which she led me to her tiny living room. There sat my father, my beloved Tati, opposite a blank wall. I ran up to him and fell on his neck, blurting out the good news that his wife, daughter and son had survived and were waiting for him at the home of Dr. Schwartz, a childhood friend. Schwartz had survived the war thanks to his mixed marriage status with a non-Jewish woman.

If my recollection of that wonderful moment serves me right, I was shocked and disappointed by my father's lack of reaction to this miraculous news. While our friend Malci stood there with tears of joy running down her cheeks, my father stood up silently and we left the little apartment. I do not remember any conversation between the two of us on our way to Dr. Schwartz's home. Nor do I remember much of the actual reunion between my father and the rest of us. Is my memory playing tricks on me? I don't know.

The next thing I do remember is our visit to our pre-war apartment on the Saská Kupa, the main street of Český Těšín. Everything there was in shambles. It seems that the Soviet occupation commandant had installed his offices in the house where previously the German SS headquarters had been. I do not know who inflicted the damage to the rooms that used to be our apartment. Some of the leather furniture in the sitting room had been bayoneted. The glass sliding doors to father's library were broken. His books had disappeared. But the worst awaited us upon our inspection of the bathroom. The bathtub was half filled with human excrement. Having had nothing but bad experiences with the soldiers of the Soviet liberation army during our repatriation home, we speculated that the soldiers, most of them natives of Mongolia, had never seen a bathtub before and assumed it was to be used as a toilet. To make a long story short, the apartment was a total loss.

In the end it was the local government that assigned to us a new apartment on the Bezručova Street, not far from the railway station. It consisted of a living room and a bedroom with kitchen. With orphaned Ilse we were now five persons in all. Edith and Ilse slept in the living room on a couple of sofas transformed into beds in the evening. I had my own bed in the parents' bedroom. Our expectations, after all we had suffered in the camps, were low. We gratefully accepted the arrangement.

Honest Malci came through as we had hoped. A few of our belongings that had been hidden by her were now returned. A couple of oil paintings of old rabbis, a small Persian throw rug, a brass lamp and a few other items made life in our new surroundings more hospitable. Also, a case of books my father was wise enough to have stored in our city museum was now returned and this, too, was somewhat of a solace for the grief we felt at the realization that all of our other belongings were gone.

Let me throw some light on the disappearance of our belongings. What I am about to report came to light a few years later when I was living in France. Edith wrote me that after my departure for France in 1947, she landed a job in the office of Český Těšín's mayor. One day she was sent out to visit a number of households in connection with a local survey. When she came to the apartment of the pharmacist Novotný, Mrs. Novotný excused herself for a moment. Going to the bedroom, she left the door ajar, which gave my sister the opportunity to peek in. What she spotted shocked her, because in there she recognized our parents' pre-war bedroom suite. The suite was easily recognizable; it consisted of several pieces made from a precious exotic South American wood. This rather unique bedroom suite had been Mutti's pride and joy; she never ceased dusting and polishing it.

As I related earlier, it was this same Mrs. Novotný whom we encountered first upon returning to our town. It was she who expressed disappointment at seeing us safely returning. Now it was clear why our reappearance disheartened her. What would become of the beautiful bedroom suite she and her husband appropriated for themselves after the Ziffers' first eviction? Would she now have to return it to the rightful owners?

## *Difficult return home*

It took my sister several years to successfully claim the bedroom suite for the family. All sorts of difficult-to-obtain documentation had to be produced to get the furniture returned. There was a lot of red tape to be dealt with. But in the end Edith succeeded. When my present wife Gail and I visited my mother and sister in Czechoslovakia in 1992, we slept in the very same beds in which, as children, my sister and I had sat at the feet of our father listening to him read to us from the classics. It was an emotional and very satisfying experience.

The purpose of my telling this incident is to show that many of our fellow inhabitants of Český Těšín – even those of Czech nationality – waited impatiently for the Jews' expulsion from the town in order to steal their belongings. Greed, accompanied by latent antisemitism, was undoubtedly one of the elements that encouraged our fellow citizens' silence when the Nazis forced us from our homes. There was much to be profited from the Jews' departure.

CHAPTER 11
# A new start in our hometown

Despite the fact that our nuclear family had been saved and now reunited, restarting life toward some kind of normalcy was not easy. My father at this point was sixty-one years old and physically as well as mentally incapable of starting on a new career. My mother, ever so protective of him, felt that he needed a long rest. This definitely was not the right time to begin a new career, what with such an effort's accompanying stresses and strains. And so father, to the best of my recollection, just sat around at home, spending a lot of time listening to the radio. Because of his pre-war presidency of the Jewish community, we were visited every so often by this or that returning Jew in quest of family and previous belongings. Sometimes these folk needed an official document from the local Jewish Religious Authority *(Židovská náboženská obec)*, of which my father, even after the war, remained the president. Naturally he was more than willing to supply these. By and large my mother saw to it that my father lived a totally stress-free leisurely life, without having to work. While I was fully aware of this state of affairs, it never occurred to me to inquire where the necessary finances for our livelihood came from. To this day I have no idea what sort of income came to us from where. What money there may have been in a pre-war savings account was no longer available; there was no pension to be had from the Czech or the German government; and there was no income from employment. My sister is the one who may have been able to tell me. Unfortunately, she died in 2001, and there remains no one whom I could ask about this puzzling matter.

My mother, the proverbial ever so loving *yiddishe mame* (Jewish mother) took care of all of us, sewing, cooking, cleaning and doing all the chores that kept her family members going. She worked tirelessly to make our new impoverished existence as livable as possible.

In my account of the concentration camp of Klettendorf I mentioned Harry Haubenstock who was a *Kapo* there. Having told my mother among other things that Harry did not come to my help in Klettendorf, she did not take to him kindly. Harry survived the war as we did and returned to his hometown of Karviná. He, with an uncle of his who survived the war – having left the country just in time – repossessed their lucrative pre-war lumber business which supplied the coal mines in the area. It was there that my sister found employment as secretary shortly after our repatriation, and I wonder whether it was the meager monies my sister earned that provided for the rent of our small apartment and the food my mother put on the table. Harry Haubenstock, who had his Jewish-sounding surname changed to Hromek after the war, was a handsome fellow, and my sister Edith was quite interested in him. The feelings, however, were not reciprocated, and Harry began courting my cousin Ilse. The two eventually married, and two daughters, Dana and Jana, were born to them.

Having been disenfranchised for all those years in the German camps, we, the younger members of the family, now tasted freedom and thoroughly enjoyed it. While there was not a whole lot of entertainment available for young people in general, there was even less to do for young Jews, what with the disappearance of pre-war Jewish youth organizations. Personally, I did not mourn this disappearance because I never enjoyed belonging. *Makkabi*, WIZO, *Ha-noar*

*Anny and Leo, Walter Ziffer's parents, 1919*

*Walter and sister Edith Ziffer, 1929*

*Uncle Emil, sister Edith, cousin Ilse, Uncle Bruno, Walter, and Uncle Oskar in front of Český Těšín's municipal building, 1931*

*1912 photograph of Český Těšín showing underpass where young Walter and his friend Jakob Katz were stoned and chased during the 1930's*

*Jewish synagogue in Cieszyn before its destruction in 1939*

*Walter Ziffer and friend George Loeffler, 1940. George did not survive the war.*

*Ziffer family, September 1940*

*Confronting the Silence*

*Nazi rally featuring Joseph Goebbels in Český Těšín, 1940*

*Walter Ziffer's passport photo, 1947*

*Carolyn Kinnard Ziffer*
(photo by Philip Schwartz)

*Gail Rosenthal*

*ha-Tzioni*, Jewish coffee houses and clubs: all these were no more. Even the Rotary Cub which used to meet in the *Slezský Dům* (Silesian House), a local hotel, in which my father was quite active as its secretary before the war, was no longer in existence. The other hotel, the "Polonia," continued to function. They even had a band, and so one evening as we walked by and thought the music to be quite inviting, Edith, Ilse with Harry at her side, and I decided to go dancing there. In the coat check room we encountered a middle-aged man who ogled us strangely; it made me feel very uncomfortable. My first thought was, "This guy had one too many." And sure enough, we did not have to wait very long before he let loose. As Harry approached the check room window to hand his overcoat to the lady, the man approached him and in a clearly inebriated voice said, "So Hitler did not succeed after all. And you Jews are back and even wanting to dance." The drunk would have to regret his words, because no sooner said than done, Harry hauled off and knocked him to the floor cold. Blood trickled from the guy's nose. We walked by the guy, all curled up on the floor, into the ballroom. A great time was had by all of us, and Harry taught me to dance that evening. Harry's quick action impressed me very much. From that evening on, I no longer held his cold behavior in Klettendorf against him.

Shortly after our arrival in Český Těšín, I was approached by the commander of the police to join the local militia. The German Nazi population of our town had been interned by the Czechs, and the old barracks that had housed our border garrison before the war – we lived on the border with Poland across the Olza River – served now as an internment camp for them. "You, Valtr (as the Czechs called me), who suffered the brunt of Nazi malfeasance, wouldn't you want to get even with the supporters of Hitler by helping us to deal with them?" This offer did not exactly turn me on, but I responded that I'd think this over and discuss it with my family. This is what I did the following evening. Pros and cons were voiced, as could be expected, but in the end two considerations were sufficiently persuasive to suggest that I accept the invitation. First, we should not alienate the Czech powers-that-be; knowing that many Czechs were antisemites themselves, we wanted to prevent them from getting the idea that we Jews were not solid citizens. Second, with the shortage of food that prevailed in those first months after the war there might be advantages to be had from such a position. And so I accepted the invitation and joined this paramilitary unit.

My first assignment, after having been given a rifle without ammunition, was to stand guard at a bakery and to oversee the distribution of bread. The queues needed to be orderly. Bullying or pushing was forbidden. It was my job to enforce such order. My standing there with the ammunition-less rifle must have put holy fear into those waiting folks, because they really behaved. And there was advantage to be had from this guard duty, because at the end of the day the baker, grateful for not having had to deal with protesters and hecklers, rewarded me with a couple of loaves for the good work I had done.

Alas this assignment did not last long. At one point I was transferred to the internment camp itself. Now the assignment was office work, keeping all sorts of statistics, arrivals and departures, etc. During this stage of my militia service I came into contact not only with the Czech guards but also with the German internees, and what I was told and actually saw I did not like. There was a constant flow of business transactions ranging from monetary bribes in exchange for temporary release, to chocolates, cigarettes or nylon stockings for sex. Far from hiding this trafficking, the Czech guards boasted to one another about their purchased amorous adventures with the German *Fräuleins*. The longer I worked there, the more disgusted I became. I desperately wished to get out of this slimy atmosphere, and discussed my options with the family. They warned me against any rash moves because after all we were Jews who should under no circumstances

## A new start in our hometown

show ingratitude to our Czech fellow citizens. It was the old mantra.

When I could no longer stand it, I decided to inform the police commandant of my decision to leave the militia service. At first the man looked at me incongruously. "Don't you enjoy seeing the situation reversed?" he asked me. "Now they are behind the barbed wire and you are outside guarding them. Does this not give you some satisfaction?" Knowing that this was not the time to complain about the repulsive hanky-panky that was going on in the camp, I tried to explain that after losing three years of my life under the Germans I needed to get an education. Offering me another position coupled with a higher rank and a pay raise, the police major tried hard to change my mind, but to no avail. In the end he relented and let me go. His parting words were, "You may regret your decision one day."

At this point I regretted nothing. To some extent I had been quite honest with the man because I truly wanted, and very badly so, to make up for lost time.

Ever since my earliest youth, my uncle Bruno was a role model to me, just second to my father. He was a chemical engineer working in a neighboring town. Every time something went wrong, say with an electrical switch or some such thing, Uncle Bruno was able to fix it. In the mid-1930s, while he was working in the chemical laboratory of the plant, a major explosion took place and boiling hot tar splashed on him. The superhot tar caused him to sustain third-degree burns on his left chest and arm. He convalesced from the mishap in our apartment, and I still remember well the physician regularly stopping by and changing his bandages. My uncle screamed as the doctor carefully removed pitch black burned skin from the injured areas with surgical pincers. While he stayed with us, perhaps six weeks or longer, he read and explained to me basic mechanical principles. What impressed me very much was that my father who, in my opinion, knew just about everything there was to know, held long conversations with Uncle Bruno, which made me think that Tati respected my uncle's knowledge in more than one discipline. The only thing Tati disagreed on was the quality of my uncle's voice. Bruno fancied himself to be a great baritone, while my father thought that his singing was closer to a wolf's howling. And so when my mother accompanied her brother on the baby grand as he sang opera arias, my father would very quietly slip out of the room. But I, who rarely if ever disagreed with my father in anything, did disagree with him concerning Bruno's quality of voice. I was always greatly impressed by his singing and theatrics and especially by his rendition of Mephistopheles' aria about "the gold that rules the world" from Gounod's *Faust*. To make a long story short, I decided at age eight or nine to become an engineer like my uncle Bruno.

This decision led me, after our return to our hometown in 1945, to visit the large automobile repair shop there, previously owned by a German by the name of Tomanek. The enterprise had been nationalized after the war, and the new administrative boss was a Czech police officer by the name of Tomáš. The German Tomanek, a much respected car repair specialist, had been kept on and, for all practical purposes, supervised the running of the facility.

Tomanek was very polite and respectful when I approached him with my request to become an automobile mechanic apprentice. He listened politely, but in the end turned me down: "There is no need for anyone at the present time." Greatly disappointed and also angry because I knew his decision was undoubtedly informed by his unrepentant Nazi dislike of Jews – he knew quite well who my father was – I happened to put my hand into my pants pocket in which I carried the keys to our house and apartment doors on a metal chain fastened to my belt. The pocket bulged a bit. No sooner had I done this than Tomanek's face turned ashen. "Wait a moment," he said. "I forgot! There actually is an opening with master mechanic Vášek. You can begin next Monday morning." I was overjoyed. Later I found out that Tomanek, who knew I had been a part of the militia at the internment

## A new start in our hometown

camp for Germans, had thought I had a pistol in my pocket and was about to threaten him with the weapon. This apparently was the cause for his quick change of mind. A few weeks later Tomanek himself was forced to join his fellow Nazis in that camp.

A lot of the garage work was filthy, and more than once when I came home in my dirty overalls with arms greasy up to my elbows, my mother would exclaim, "*Ach Du lieber Gott,* do you really have to get yourself that dirty?" Scrubbing with a generous amount of soap took care of the condition.

Doing my apprenticeship under Mr. Vášek, who had acquired his own automotive repair expertise in the Tatra automobile works, was well worth getting greasy. The man knew his business admirably and was at the same time an excellent pedagogue. Before long he entrusted me with jobs which apprentices with longer service records than mine would not have been allowed to perform. I must confess that I pulled a number of major booboos during the apprenticeship, which cost the company money. But both Mr. Vášek and Mr. Tomáš, knowing where I was coming from, forgave me. I loved every bit of this two-year-long learning process. Years later when I lived in the U.S., my father wrote me that Mr. Vášek inquired after my well-being every time they met in the street.

It is not an exaggeration when I say that I rode the crest of a wave of happiness those days. And it was not just the shop work that gave me a lot of satisfaction. A middle-aged Jewish couple, the Teichners, had moved into our town, and with them came their adopted daughter Helen, sixteen years old. I called her Helenka, a Czech form of endearment for Helen. And oh, was she beautiful with her golden hair, her pearl-like white teeth, an aquiline nose, her large expressive eyes and, last but not least, her pretty physical shape. When I first met her in our little apartment, the family had come to inquire of my father whether life in our town was livable for Jews and would he recommend they settle there. I have no idea about the conversation that ensued because I was fully occupied taking stock of Helenka. It was love at first sight. My father's response to their question must have been in the affirmative, because they took an apartment in town. My mother, quick to size up other people's looks, was quite taken by Helenka's. "She is a beautiful girl," mother would say, quickly adding, "just too bad that she has such heavy legs. But Walti, you are right, she is gorgeous." Well, I did not mind the heavy legs in the least. To me she looked flawless.

Because her German was not good, I offered to give her lessons. As she sat at the table and read out loud for me, I would bend over her, touching her lovely hair and inhaling its fragrance. After the lesson I often accompanied her home. By and by I started visiting at the Teichners on a regular basis. Helenka was quite a flirt and, in my opinion, much more experienced than I in matters of sex. I remember the time when she stood at the window and I sat on the armrest of the couch right next to her. Suddenly she began slowly raising her dress just short of showing me what must have been the triangle of her pubic hair, teasing me with, "Look, Walti, I am not wearing any underwear!" I find it hard to believe that I made no move to draw her to me and perhaps explore. Shy as I was then, I did not know how to respond with anything other than a giggling and embarrassed "Oh?"

We had good times together frequenting the small movie theater in our town, going for long walks together, smooching, eating ice cream and dancing to old German records playing on a Victrola in our living room. I had found the old record player somewhere discarded and had repaired it. When the turntable lost its élan and started to turn ever more slowly, I opened up the mechanical works of the little music machine and lubricated it with, of all things, melted margarine. To my great surprise – it shouldn't have been one since I was a mechanic – the turntable soon came to a halt. Only then did I come to the less than brilliant conclusion that melted margarine, once cooled, takes on its original semi-solid state. So back I went to the

## A new start in our hometown

inner works of the Victrola, cleaning it with gasoline and lubricating it with fine machine oil taken home from the garage. And then Ilse, Edith, Helenka and I began dancing again in the tiny area between the living room and my parents' bedroom. In those days our expectations from life were very modest indeed.

It was 1946. Dark clouds gathered once again on the political horizon. Everything pointed to a Communist takeover. It was clear to me that if this took place I would be drafted into the army. I said to myself, "I must not let this happen to me because, counting the time from the Polish occupation through the German misery in the concentration camps, I have already lost eight years which, under normal conditions, I would have spent in school." And so I implored my parents to help me leave this threatening situation in a very vulnerable Czechoslovak Republic before it was too late. Unlike service in the U.S. Armed Forces, where a soldier has opportunities for education, being drafted into a Czech Communist army would have meant three years of doing nothing constructive – a total loss.

My mother tried to talk me out of the move. I well understood why she resisted, often with tears in her eyes. "Walti, we were separated for three years. Wasn't that enough? Now that our *lieber Gott* reunited us, should we not try hard to remain together?" She was such a loving and caring mother. But my father knew the danger inherent in my remaining in Czechoslovakia and understood my fears. If there was one single thing he hoped for, it was that I become a well-educated person and make a constructive contribution to society. Thanks to the connections his old schoolmate Dr. Zelmanowitsch had in Prague, the latter procured for me a Czech passport and a seven-day visa for Paris, France. Another old friend of father's, a veterinarian practicing in Paris, assured him that he would take me under his care for a few days until he made the necessary contacts with a Jewish orphanage in Champigny-sur-Marne, an eastern suburb of Paris. This orphanage for Holocaust orphans, run under the auspices of the

*Organisation-Securité-Enfants (OSE)*, would become my temporary destination in France and a place of transit on my way to America. Mrs. Kandl, a former Jewish inhabitant of Teschen, directed the *Maison OSE* and assured my parents that I would find a good temporary home with her. Uncle Bruno, who had married and left Europe two days before the outbreak of the war, was now established in Nashville, Tennessee, managing the technical aspects of a Jewish-owned gasoline refinery. He solemnly promised to do everything in his power to facilitate my immigration to the U.S. once I got to France. I would then live with his family until I was able to stand on my own feet. This was a generous offer considering that he and his wife, Marianne, had two small children.

The arrangements my father made cost a lot of money because the Czech travel documents had to be bought. At that time it was virtually impossible to procure legal documents for a person of my age in view of the already announced coming military draft. At the time it did not occur to me to ask questions about the provenance of the monies that were spent in this connection. I was young and adventurous, and so all of it sounded good to me. Despite my mother's tearful protests, the date of my departure was set for February 27, 1947, and there was no backing away from that decision. The ease with which I decided to leave town was facilitated by the fact that the Teichner family with Helenka had left for Israel a few months before.

The time for my departure arrived, and the goodbyes were very difficult. Everybody wept, and I noticed even on my father's cheek a tear or two running down to his moustache. Edith, my sister, ever the courageous and decisive one, pressed on to get these woeful moments behind us as fast as possible. Picking up the old beat-up suitcase that had been carefully packed by my mother with a few shirts, an extra pair of pants, socks, handkerchiefs, extra underwear and the ever-ubiquitous chunks of salami and bread, Edith sort of pushed me out of the little entrance hall onto the staircase. "Let's go. Let's go now!"

## A new start in our hometown

she insisted. My heart beat hard and my chest felt terribly empty as I realized this was the first step toward a totally unknown future.

Our apartment was quite close to the railroad station. Edith's last question was, "Walti, are you sure you have your passport and train ticket?" I nodded affirmatively, and at that moment the train arrived in the station. There was a hasty parting embrace at which even the ever-courageous Edith wiped her eyes. She then helped me carry the heavy suitcase up the steps to my train compartment and quickly left without looking back. The station master's whistle blew, and he raised the departure standard in the direction of the locomotive. The rushing sound of the steam intensified, and the train starting moving. I stood at the window waving to Edith, who with distance gradually became smaller and smaller until she vanished from my sight. My chest felt empty and at the same time terribly heavy with anxiety. It was the same feeling I had experienced for the first time in my life looking out of the window in the Sosnowitz *Dulag*, seeing my parents, Edith and Ilse below in the street, slowly walking out of my sight. Once again I felt terribly alone, sad and scared.

In my mind I imagined by mother – Mutti – imploring her *lieber Gott* to accompany and protect her son into this new unknown. My courage faltered. I swallowed hard. Once again I felt like "little Walti" and wished I had my mother's protective arms wrapped around me.

CHAPTER 12
# The chess game

The train stopped at a good many stations and my compartment gradually filled up. There was a lengthy halt in Prague where cars were being shuffled around and a new locomotive attached. Our itinerary was to be Prague, Dresden and then – with a few stops through West Germany to Strasbourg and then west to Paris – arrival at Paris's *Gare de l'Est* (East Station). It was there that Tati's old friend, the veterinary doctor, was to pick me up.

Six people filled the two wooden benches that faced each other, and there was no conversation. All of these men were seemingly farm workers, judging from their attire and their heavy muddy shoes. From time to time one would open his lunch box, silently extract a chunk of dark bread, and with his pocket knife slice off a bit of sausage. The hot coffee – or was it soup? – steamed from the inverted screw-on thermos cover serving as cup. Watching these guys eat made my mouth water. I, too, could have had the pleasure of my goodies had they not been packed in the large suitcase that rested on the shelf above my seat. With all these rough-looking men in the compartment, and me being the youngest, smallest and weakest, I just could not bring myself to wrestling that heavy suitcase down and unpacking my food under everybody's eyes. And so I sat there staring out of the window, forced to inhale the delicious aromas emanating from their sausages. It was getting lighter outside. Day was dawning as we approached the border with Germany.

Knowing that my passport with the stamped-in visa was not the genuine thing, I became increasingly worried about the imminent border passport control. What if the examining official detected that these were false papers? As the train slowed down, entering the border station, I felt the heat rising to my cheeks. Would the examining border guards recognize my nervous agitation? And if detected as holder of a false passport, what would the fallout be?

At that very moment the compartment door flew open and a Czech soldier standing in its frame said to us, "Who in this compartment plays chess?" At first there was silence and then, very hesitatingly, I ventured, "I do."

My father, a fairly seasoned chess player, began teaching me this royal game when I was four or five. We began with end games with just a few pieces on the board, and then graduated to ever-larger set-ups. We worked on chess challenges in the newspaper that read "three moves and checkmate." We replayed championship games and tried to outguess the masters.

"Get your baggage and follow me!" When my efforts to get the large suitcase down seemed too slow to the burly soldier, he came over and with one sweeping motion got it down. He carried the suitcase and preceded me. I followed through two or three cars, ending up in the first-class portion of the train. There the soldier threw open the sliding door of a compartment, and for the first time in my life I saw what traveling in first class was like. There were only four seats, and their upholstery was plush red velvet. On the backrest of each seat, at the height of the passenger's head, was attached a little crocheted doily. Everything was very elegant. But what stunned me was that the three occupants of the seats were high-ranking Czech officers. Recognizing the military officers' rank insignia, I realized

## The chess game

that the solidly built, gray-haired man by the window was a general. The soldier lifted my heavy suitcase onto one of the shelves overhead, pointed to the empty seat opposite the general, and said, "Sit here." He then kicked his heels together, saluted the general, and exited. The next thing I heard was the general's voice: "OK, young man, play!"

It all seemed totally unreal. With all the excitement of the last few minutes, I had no time to worry about the fake passport in my breast pocket. The general opened the chess game by advancing the king pawn, and I responded with mine.

Soon after, the train screeched to a halt. I knew we had arrived at the border station. I said to myself, "Just play. Do your best." Yet, at the same time, I could not help hearing compartment doors sliding open and being shut with a bang. It was impossible not to hear the rough voices of soldiers giving commands, and unhappy imploring voices of passengers who were seemingly forced to leave the train. There was quite a bit of tumult. With one eye on the chessboard and the other noticing the heads of folk running to and fro outside, it was difficult to maintain concentration. The passport, once again, made itself noticeable in the pocket of my jacket.

And then it happened as I had feared all along. The sliding door of our compartment was rather violently drawn open, and three border policemen stood there: Russian, Czech and German. I still see before me the Russian officer with his submachine gun slung over his shoulder. I froze.

But now something totally unexpected occurred. Before these men could even open their mouths, the general dismissed them with a deprecating movement of his right hand, as if to say, "Get out, will you? Can't you see I am occupied?" The three soldiers immediately kicked their heels together, smartly saluted, and slid the door shut. They were gone and I was safe. I was tempted to give my savior a big hug, but there was a chess game to be played, and it was not long before the train began rolling again. The worst was over.

Now, if you are curious about that chess game, let me tell you that I lost, but honorably so.

Several years later someone, after hearing me tell this story, suggested that I send it to the *Reader's Digest* for publication. I did that, only to receive their response to the effect that my story could not possibly be true and therefore could not be considered for their category of "True Stories."

CHAPTER 13

# Champigny-sur-Marne and Paris

The train steamed into the Paris East Station and, as promised, my father's boyhood friend the veterinarian was there to pick me up. Hearing him call for Walter Ziffer enormously relieved my anxiety, because without him and without being able to say anything beyond *"bonjour"* in French, I would have been hopelessly lost in the huge strange city. The hustle and bustle at the enormous station intimidated me. It was truly awesome. Český Těšín's population was about fifteen thousand; that of Paris was in the millions.

My stay in Paris was very brief, just long enough to be taken out one evening to the Folies Bergère, the world-famous theater, where beautiful women perform to this day almost nude. All this impressed and also aroused me, of course. The next day the good man, after making a couple of phone calls, took me by the excellent Metro subway to the system's eastern end station. There he bought a ticket for me and placed me on the bus to Champigny, an eastern suburb of the huge city. The ride took about forty minutes. Upon arrival at the Champigny bus stop, Madame Kandl, the *directrice* of the OSE orphanage, cigarette in hand, welcomed me. Once again, this was a moment of great relief for me, the penniless immigrant.

The ride in Madame Kandl's old clunker took but a few minutes to the *rue* Guy Moquet, a steep winding street at the foot of which stood the large OSE mansion, surrounded by a fenced-in garden. It is here that the first French chapter of my life began.

My entrance into the house was tumultuously greeted by a noisy group of young boys of various ages and sizes. They all crowded around me. "Who are you? Where are you from? How old are you?" bombarded me from all sides. Rescued from this friendly but rather violent onslaught by a stern looking young man at whose appearance the boys let go of me, I was shown to the house office by Monsieur Bott, the resident tutor of the orphanage boys. It was he who taught the basics of the French language to all the new arrivals whose home prior to World War II had been in eastern Europe, primarily Poland and western Russia. After enrolling them in French high schools, so-called *lycées*, he continued helping them with their studies in everything from social studies to physics. Monsieur Bott, a severe-looking but kind disciplinarian – a Jew – lived with his wife and little baby boy on the premises of the orphanage.

Because I really was not a Holocaust orphan, both my parents having survived, a lodging arrangement outside the orphanage had to be found. Thanks to Madame Kandl, the problem was quickly resolved. Madame Bérard, a plump kind-looking divorcee who took care of the house's laundry and owned a house just one block away, offered to rent me a room under her roof. The tiny room was literally under the roof in the attic, adjoining a larger space whose interior was largely unfinished. There was neither running water nor a toilet up there. For these, one had to descend to the level below. My room measured around twelve by twelve feet and was just large enough to hold a bed, a small table with chair, and a small cupboard. A tiny window gave onto the adjoining roofs. The rest of the panorama was sky. Naturally I was expected to pay a modest sum for this accommodation.

But to be able to do so, I had to find employment. Again Madame Kandl rose to the challenge with aplomb. Having been informed by my father prior to my arrival about the two-year automobile mechanic apprenticeship I had served in my hometown, she had contacted Champigny's largest repair garage, Girardin & Fils. And so a few days after my arrival, after having settled into my little cell at Madame Bérard's house, Madame Kandl and I set out to visit Monsieur Girardin, the owner. He, an elderly man, and his son Maurice were friendly people. They listened to Madame Kandl's eloquent pleading for a job for me and kindly arranged for me to begin working there the following week. They actually needed an extra mechanic, and so it seems that I had arrived just in time. The problem I was not aware of was that Madame Kandl had introduced me as a full-blown mechanic rather than a mere apprentice mechanic who had not yet been graduated into full mechanic-hood.

The mechanic I worked with completely trusted my competence, and one day told me to repair a leaking water pump on a truck engine. This meant unscrewing four bolts, making a new gasket, placing some semi-liquid sealer on it, and then reattaching the pump. Taking off the pump was no problem, nor was the preparation of the gasket. What went wrong, however, was that in attaching the pump to the engine body by fastening one of the bolts, I stripped one of the threads and the bolt broke off. Now had I simply informed my mechanic about the mishap, he would have surely understood and assisted me in repairing the problem. But I was afraid – an attitude undoubtedly acquired in the German camps. There, a mishap of this kind would have been quickly penalized by severe beatings or worse. With the German hell barely two years behind me, I had not yet overcome the fear of being severely punished for a wrongdoing. Naively I thought I'd get by with a cover-up. Putting some special glue on the end of the bolt, I inserted it so that it gave the impression of being securely fastened. I pretended the job was done. But then happened what I should have foreseen. Once the engine was started with the radiator filled with water, the water gushed out from the area of the gasket that had not been properly fastened because of the broken bolt. My sham was discovered, and I felt terribly ashamed. Amazingly, neither my mechanic nor young Monsieur Girardin fussed with me. I think they understood my dilemma, knowing where I was coming from. They merely exhorted me sternly in French – speeches which I understood only partly – never to repeat this kind of deceitful action again. Also, my pay was reduced in accordance with my demotion to reflect my new position as mechanic-assistant. These were good people. From here on things went smoothly, and the money I earned more than covered my expenses with Madame Bérard as well as the monthly payment to the orphanage for my meals.

Champigny was to be only a transitional stay on my way to the United States. With the American Embassy's location close to the Place de la Concorde in the heart of Paris, it became very inconvenient for me to keep track of what was happening with my emigration efforts. Upon my request, the American Jewish Joint Distribution Committee, or in short the JOINT, had taken my case under their advisement.

Waiting for that American visa was not unlike "waiting for Godot." I became terribly impatient. My main hope was a young woman named Ruth Baeck, a fellow ex-Czech citizen now residing in Paris and working for the JOINT. When I came to know her better, she told me that she was a niece of the famous Rabbi Leo Baeck, the renowned "angel of Theresienstadt," the infamous Czech transit concentration camp. Before being deported by the Nazis, Rabbi Baeck had been the chief rabbi of Berlin.

Ruth Baeck at the JOINT was tireless in advancing my cause with the American Embassy in Paris. But just in case her efforts did not pan out, I also contacted Israel's Haganah recruiting office in Paris, who welcomed me with open arms. Haganah, the Israeli Defense Forces, were in need of manpower in their struggle to achieve independence from Great Britain. I registered with them and was assured that before long I would be notified with regard to my being called up and shipped out to Palestine.

My uncle Bruno in Nashville, Tennessee, true to his promise made to my parents, made every effort to help me join his family in America. He sent me every month a few dollars so that, when the time came, I would be able to pay for my trans-Atlantic boat passage, estimated to cost around $150.

Sometime in early December of 1948, the Haganah informed me that I would be shipped out around the middle of the month. They suggested I prepare myself for the trip. The call to go to Palestine to help with the Jewish struggle for independence came as a great relief to me, and I began packing the few belongings I had. I also informed my folks back in Czechoslovakia that my departure for Palestine was imminent, and I wondered how my parents and sister would receive the news. Would they be happy about it, or would they regret that my emigration to the USA aborted? Ruth, in any case, advised me against it. She felt certain that the arrival of the United States visa was now around the corner. And she was right. A few days after my contact with the Haganah, she phoned to inform me that the visa had, in fact, arrived and that I was to meet with the U.S. Consul General the following day.

What a difficult decision to make! I remember lying awake the following night, smoking like a chimney and cogitating about the pros and cons of the two options that lay before me. By sunrise I had made my decision: the USA.

PART THREE
*America*

# Introduction

From the day in February 1947 when I said goodbye to family and native country and set out for America and an unknown future, my life had many ups and downs and basic reorientations. My first marriage, which made me the father of four children, brought joy but also heartbreak. The professional change from engineering to the study and teaching of theology has been a fascinating adventure. The ongoing search for God, ending in atheism, has brought sadness as well as liberation. My discovery of what I consider true love has given me valuable insights into what life should be all about. Experiences in the field of education have persuaded me that if there is hope for a better world, it must come through better education of both young and old. Given this varied past that has led me to the last paragraphs of the last chapter of my life, and having distilled this past to the best of my ability, it is now my intention to share this distillate or legacy with the reader.

There is much here that I do not fully understand myself. There is much here that defies explanation. But is this not the case for every person's life? To some, the linking of events and their unfolding seems predestined by a higher power. As others see it, and that includes me, things simply happen, both on the individual and collective level. It is only in retrospect that we find meaning in the flow of it all, or so at least we think. I ask: must there be meaning in events? Can we not accept the randomness of life? Can we not accept the accidental nature of all being?

One of William Blake's poems comes to mind:

*Every Night and every Morn*
*Some to Misery are Born*
*Every Morn and every Night*
*Some are Born to sweet Delight*
*Some are Born to sweet Delight*
*Some are Born to Endless Night*

Blake's choice of the word "some" in the poem suggests randomness or the universe's indifference to human well-being or to its opposite, human suffering. John Schaar, a political theorist at the University of California at Berkeley, writes, "The future is not some place we are going, but one we are creating. The paths are not to be found, but made. And the activity of making them changes both the maker and their destination." Reality, I think, lies somewhere between these two wise sayings. So then, what have I learned from life? It is with "fear and trembling" (a Kierkegaardian expression) that I am setting out on the adventure of trying to discern in the following pages a few important insights gained from my past life.

## CHAPTER 14
# Nashville, Tennessee

**AMERICAN HIGH SCHOOL**

It is not easy to compensate for the loss of five years of one's life. Between September 1939 when World War II began and my liberation by the Soviet army at Waldenburg concentration camp on May 8, 1945, I lost six years of what would have been a normal secondary education. During the first three of those, my father, cultured educator that he was, tried hard to advance my sister's and my education. He did this despite his painful responsibility as head of the Nazi-established *Judenrat* or Jewish representation. This remarkable man, who had never set foot on English-speaking soil but taught himself English by listening to BBC radio broadcasts, set out to teach me some English and basic German grammar by translating Ellery Queen's *The Tragedy of X* and a Somerset Maugham short story. With only five years of elementary school education behind me, I was typing these on his Remington portable typewriter.

With this small educational baggage, I came to America and enrolled at Hume-Fogg Technical and Vocational High School in Nashville. By a tour de force on the part of Marianne, my uncle's wife, and the hard work of the team of fine teachers, I was able to graduate from twelfth grade in less than one year. I then enrolled at Vanderbilt University's engineering school. Given the few high school credits I possessed at graduation, Dean "Fireball" Lewis was very reluctant to accept me into his engineering school. But thanks to my aunt's good looks and perhaps a bit of flirting, he took a chance on me. Never could I have made it through the difficult curriculum without the help of my uncle, who was a chemical engineer.

### ENCOUNTER WITH THE JEWISH COMMUNITY OF NASHVILLE

It was Uncle Bruno, himself an immigrant from Czechoslovakia, who facilitated my immigration to the United States. Having registered with the U.S. immigration quota system before the war, he was fortunate to leave the country, after marriage to Marianne, two days before World War II broke out. They settled in Nashville, Tennessee, where he became manager of a small oil refinery. Bruno and Marianne had two lovely little children, Jimmy and Lisa, and a mutt named Bushy.

My first encounter with my American family's Jewish friends about two weeks after my arrival in Nashville went something like this. I sat in the living room of the modest duplex on Clifton Lane. In a half-circle around me sat some of Marianne's friends. Following a brief introduction by Marianne of her twenty-one-year-old nephew, she suggested that the guests ask me questions. "What do you think of America? How do you like American girls? Is American food better than European food?" etc. My English was inadequate. The clothing I wore contrasted poorly with the ladies' attire. I was shy and intimidated. I had expected questions about the family I had left behind. I had thought they would inquire after my Holocaust experience. After all, this was 1948! Only three years had gone by since the greatest ever catastrophe had befallen world Jewry. And here I was put on display as one who had escaped that hell but was now being asked utterly trivial questions. What was wrong with these American Jews, I wondered.

In a way, this was an ominous beginning for my future relationship with the Jews of Nashville – not that I realized it at that time, of course. When some time later, after I had acquired a better grasp

## Nashville, Tennessee

of English, I began teaching young people at Vine Street Temple, the Jewish Reform Congregation worship venue of Nashville, it also struck me that even their rabbi never asked about my Holocaust experiences. Again I wondered about these people's silence. Weren't they interested in what had happened to their counterparts in Europe?

As a youngster and one who was Jewishly rather uneducated, I was unable to understand these Jews' reluctance to ask questions. In all probability, most of these silent Jewish men and women would not have been able to explain to themselves their hesitation to ask Holocaust-related questions. Their silence was unconscious, I think, and the reasons for it ran deep. It was the silence of Jewish trauma. There may also have been feelings of guilt that American Jewry had not done enough to help their European brothers and sisters during their time of supreme anguish. Despite these American Jewish people's only minimal acquaintance with their own Jewish history, they were aware of the traditionally taught special bond the people of Israel had with the biblical God, a bond that promises love and protection from *HaShem* (Hebrew circumlocution for the name of God), the almighty and all-loving God above. They and I thought that this God would protect us Jews, his children, in a world that did not seem to like us. But then came the Holocaust with its total unbridled brutality, which destroyed all thought of security. No wonder that it was in the midst of this hell that we Jews began having doubts about God's faithfulness. Wasn't Jewish silence after Auschwitz an expression of bewilderment? Was Jewish silence an expression of feeling abandoned both by humanity and by God?

Of course my own feelings participated in this dramatic Jewish conundrum. On the one hand, I wanted to be asked about my Holocaust-related past. Jews have been taught for centuries to remember (Hebrew: *zakhor*), never to forget. On the other hand, however, I wanted desperately to forget. For the following fourteen years, I actually succeeded in forgetting. Even though I did begin telling my story to my children when they began asking questions at the dinner table in the 1960's, it was reading Elie Wiesel's book *Night* that deeply disturbed me. His evocations sent me back to my own recollections of hell and woke me from my self-induced Holocaust-related nap.

### VANDERBILT UNIVERSITY AND CAROLYN

It was at Vanderbilt in Social Science 101 that I found myself sitting next to a pretty girl by the name of Carolyn Kinnard. She was the daughter of a large-scale farmer in Franklin, a town south of Nashville. I sat on her left side, her boyfriend to her right. We were listening to Professor Bellissery, a skinny little man sitting on his desk with his feet dangling. He spoke about the post-World War I formation of some of the central European nations, of which my country was one. When he ended his lecture, he turned toward me and said, "Do you agree with this interpretation of European history, Mr. Ziffer?" Knowing little about the subject, what could I do but nod my head in agreement and say, "Yes." My "fame" in that course was instantaneous.

Carolyn must also have noticed what a "celebrity" sat to her left. From that time on, we began talking to each other and meeting for common study in the library. It took me a long time to invite her for a cup of coffee at Vanderbilt's bookstore. In a conversation there, I learned that she was also taking a course in French, so I offered to be of help to her. Centennial Park, with the famous replica of Athens' Parthenon, was frequently our meeting place. There, sitting on a bench together, we rehearsed conjugations of French verbs, and it came to holding hands.

As our relationship deepened, I began thinking about a possible future with her. But I was a Jew and she a Christian belonging to the non-instrumental Church of Christ, the mostly Southern-based fundamentalist Christian denomination. I realized that the religious barrier between the two of us would be nearly impossible to overcome. We lived in America's Bible Belt. The problem often deprived me of sleep. One night as I lay there desperately trying to find a solution to my dilemma, I came up with the "brilliant" idea of how to get rid of my religion that stood in the way of my happiness. It would be a lie about my background that would save me. In reality, you see, I really was not a Jew. I was the son of a Christian couple who had lost their lives in an automobile accident. The wonderful people who adopted me and my sister happened to be Jews and good friends of my birth parents. This explained my Jewish upbringing and my Holocaust experience. To me, all this sounded reasonable enough in terms of an explanation. This will work, I convinced myself. Telling a lie would be my way of entering the American Christian world and being accepted there.

The dishonesty of misleading a person I loved and her family, whom I respected, caused me no lack of sleep. The Holocaust experience had made it easy to lie even after liberation. Lying persuasively had become a necessity for survival in the concentration camps. "Did you break the handle of this hammer?" – a question asked by the German crew chief – had to be answered with a lie, or else. "Did you snitch to the Nazi guard on _____ who tried to smuggle a letter out of the camp?" The response had to be a firm "No," or else. Lying had become a normal part of our instinctual drive for survival – a habit. Once acquired, it was not easy to quit. Besides, in my particular case, probably unconsciously so, it was a productive and even noble instrument to combat the religious bigotry I was facing. After all, why should this matter of religion keep lovers apart? Neither a superficial nor a trite question! Therefore, when the opportunity offered itself, I explained my "real" religious background. Carolyn, I think, believed me and relayed the information to her parents. Whether or not Mr. and Mrs. Brown C. Kinnard believed this hackneyed story, I do not know. In any case, I was now invited to their home. When, after our marriage, I confessed to Carolyn that I had lied, she forgave me.

A subsequent event persuaded me that my action had been right. In need of new clothing, I chose buying a suit in a Franklin store. To my disappointment, the clerks were not at all helpful to me. I got the impression that they would have preferred my going elsewhere. In disgust with the poor service, I left the store and related my unpleasant adventure to Carolyn's father. He made a quick phone call and then advised me to try the store again. I did just that, and now was amazed how this time the two men, in an effort to help me choose and try on the clothing, practically stumbled over each other in their efforts to be amiable and helpful. The transformation of the service was downright miraculous. Was it because they had realized that their suspicion of me being a Jew was found to be wrong? Mr. Kinnard surely would not have reprimanded them in favor of a Jewish customer who felt maltreated.

Uncle Bruno and MaryAnn (Americanized form of the former German Marianne) staunchly opposed my dating of Carolyn Kinnard. Upon hearing the name of my new girlfriend for the first time, they were horrified. Was it not a person named Kinnard who owned the beautiful Willow Plunge swimming pool, frequented by many Vanderbilt students, whose entrance had a sign that read, "Negroes and Jews not welcome"? They were right. This was one of Carolyn's relatives. They thought I had lost my mind, while I was convinced that true love would triumph over religious bigotry.

In retrospect I understand both perspectives. MaryAnn had lost both her parents, and Bruno his four brothers, in the Holocaust. I, who had spent three years in Nazi camps and had escaped being murdered by the ferociously antisemitic Nazis, was now dating a Christian girl related to an American antisemite. "What else but pure folly now possesses our nephew, whom we brought over to live with us, to commit this kind of blunder?" must have been my uncle's and aunt's justified question.

It was interesting and a pleasure to accompany Carolyn to church services at Hillsboro Church of Christ in Nashville. Brother Batsell Barrett Baxter was an excellent preacher. The congregants were extremely welcoming. On a Wednesday evening after a prayer

## Nashville, Tennessee

meeting, when the "invitation" was given, I went forward and was baptized. Carolyn, who had hoped this would happen, was very pleased. In retrospect, this spontaneous act is fully understandable to me. As already indicated, my Judaic baggage at the time of my arrival in the United States at age 21 was virtually non-existent; my father – and major role model – was not a ritually practicing religious Jew. Also, my lack of positive communication with the Jewish community of Nashville soured the relationship between me and the rabbi of the congregation. Most importantly, my overwhelming desire to marry Carolyn, a Christian girl, worked unconsciously within me and over-ruled any hesitations I may have had to leave the sphere of Jewishness. I am certain that theological considerations, at that stage in my life, played no part in my decision making.

When I came home flushed with excitement from what I had done, and the Borgers (my uncle's surname was Borger) heard my story, all hell broke loose. From that moment on, tension between them and me overshadowed our daily life under the same roof.

That summer something else very important happened. During a physics course at Peabody College (now part of Vanderbilt University), I met Burton Grant. We hit it off. Out of the blue, Burton asked me one day if I would be willing to move in with his mother to be "her surrogate son" during his years of absence in Memphis where he would be studying medicine at the University of Tennessee. Burton was worried about her living alone in the big mansion. Given the unbearable daily stress at my uncle's place, I accepted the invitation without hesitation. The following Sunday, while the Borger family had gone for a ride, I threw my stuff into the 1938 black Buick sedan I had acquired from a school friend, left an explanatory note in the Borger mailbox, and drove to the Grants' beautiful home. With this move a new chapter in my life had begun.

*Confronting the Silence*

**INLAND EQUIPMENT COMPANY, GRADUATION, ON TO DAYTON**

My departure from the Borgers must have been a heavy blow to the family. As I learned from my cousin Lisa decades later, her brother was devastated and, years later as an adult, declared me dead. Lesson learned: holding grudges can be a foolish and destructive matter.

Life in Mrs. Zell Grant's house was good. As her son Burton had imagined, I ran errands, washed her car, mowed the lawn, built a tool shed, drove her to church, etc. She cared for me like a doting mother. Dinner was waiting when I came home, often late in the evening. My independent income came from being a draftsman at the Inland Equipment Company in Nashville, an industrial outfit producing replacement mufflers and army ordnance such as practice bazooka rockets, airplane tachometer testers, etc. The owner and the manager were kind to me even after I once made a drafting error that resulted in scrapping several thousand machine gun firing pins. My modest pay for the after-school hours spent in the factory sufficed for Vanderbilt tuition and incidentals.

When in June 1953 Carolyn and I married at the Kinnard family's Franklin home, Zell Grant was there. Because I still had one year of study ahead of me, her wedding gift was free occupancy of a large room with attached kitchenette and bathroom for one year. To honor her, Carolyn and I named our first child Elizabeth Zell. Little did I know then that the same Zell Grant would turn out to be the grandmother of Amy Grant, the famous gospel and country music singer who has become our friend.

After I graduated from Vanderbilt's engineering school, Carolyn, our first child and I moved to Dayton, Ohio, where I was offered the position of design engineer at the Inland Manufacturing Division of General Motors. Dayton was a General Motors town at the time, with five divisions of the huge industrial giant operating there, employing close to one hundred thousand people. I had Uncle Bruno, the chemical engineer, as my childhood role model, and now

## Nashville, Tennessee

I had become an engineer myself! Far from being a brilliant student, the totality of my performance at Vanderbilt rated probably a C+. I actually loathed studying calculus, differential equations and thermodynamics, the latter being the only course I flunked and had to repeat. Nonetheless, I became senior project engineer for the rather sophisticated design and manufacture of automotive door and window seals that keep vehicle passengers dry when it rains. Some creative work in that field, as also in the field of steering wheel and windshield washer design, earned me four U.S. patents that, with a crisp one dollar note tucked into a paper pocket of the patent grant, rest in one of my memorabilia suitcases to this day.

This said, I found the technical work rather uninspiring. The almost weekly trips to Detroit, GM's technical center where the doors I had to seal were designed, became a nuisance. As a participant in the process of establishing prices for our products, I was expected to sit in on sales department meetings. These discussions, resulting in huge markups, especially for replacement parts, turned me off. The decisive criterion for the pricing was to go as high as the public would bear. We had the customer over the barrel. I became seriously disenchanted with this unethical process. Needless to say, this was naiveté on my part.

While in engineering school I had taken an elective course in philosophy taught by Professor Samuel Stumpf, a brilliant scholar. Every session opened my mind to questions and problems about the fundamental nature of reality, existence, knowledge, values, ethics, etc. It was probably in his class that I discovered my love for *philosophia*, Greek for love of wisdom. Little did I know then that this love for wisdom and search for truth would lead me back to school and to a new profession – a profession which, thanks to Professor Stumpf's challenging lectures at Vanderbilt, promised to help me not only understand, but also deal creatively with issues and problems that I would undoubtedly encounter in the future.

In Dayton, Carolyn and I began attending a Disciples of Christ church, a somewhat more liberal offshoot from the Church of Christ where I had converted. It was a very friendly church led by one Harry Smith, a good preacher and sensitive minister. His theology credentials were from the Graduate School of Theology of Oberlin College in Oberlin, Ohio, a well-known progressive college. The study of engineering taught me to think through issues logically, so I was surprised at what happened one evening when Harry came to visit us (physicians and ministers still made house calls in those days). He noticed on our living room bookshelf a book dealing with evolution, and he became a bit unsettled. "So you folks believe in evolution?" he inquired. "Yes, of course. Who doesn't?" I responded. "What about the Genesis creation?" he continued. A lengthy conversation on the subject ensued, and I became aware that Harry was taken aback by our position. At one point he pulled from his pocket a little satchel and emptied its contents into the hollow of his hand. A quick glance told me that these were parts of a disassembled pocket watch. In a sort of triumphant manner, he held out his hand and said, "Now then, my friends, would these parts of the watch ever come together by themselves?" and, after a brief pause, "How long do you think it would take before these parts started ticking?" I admit, Carolyn and I were stumped regarding an answer. Harry clearly noticed our bafflement. He had won the argument for the moment. "You see, Walter," he continued, "revelation often trumps science. God was there first and knows best." Our conversation from here on became a bit forced, and Harry left. I knew instinctively that there was a flaw in his argument, but I was not able to find the chink in his armor. I had studied engineering and not biology. Self-education over the following years helped me fill the lacunae that had come with skipping middle and high school.

 The five years in Dayton were good years, but professionally, despite my climbing the ladder of success on the job, I felt unfulfilled. There was more to life than coming up with ever better door and window seals for cars. Also, the somewhat tainted figure of Harry

## Nashville, Tennessee

Smith since our evolution discussion weighed on me. It was time for a change. I taught a class of young couples at Harry Smith's First Christian Church in Kettering, a suburb of Dayton, and I felt energized to take a first step toward a new career. Scholarship, education and ministry gradually revealed themselves as the objectives I should be pursuing. The five years with General Motors had been useful in my process of maturation, but now, feeling fully supported by Carolyn, I took the plunge. Graduate studies in theology beckoned to me as the new path into the future. Advised and recommended by Harry Smith, I enrolled at the Graduate School of Theology at Oberlin College.

One incident reinforced my decision to take this step, and held a clue as to my unique calling. Every summer in Harry Smith's church we were urged to volunteer as counselors at Camp Christian, a denominational youth camp located in Magnetic Springs, Ohio. Attracted by this opportunity to serve and to learn, I volunteered. On arrival, I was assigned a cabin with twenty boys. The program was typical for such a gathering of youngsters: morning worship, camp and cabin cleanup, study, physical exercise, races, meals, games, singing around the campfire and so on. All of it was good, clean fun. I remember a "best looking leg" contest between the counselors one evening, which I won and was subsequently teased about. The following morning in the outside shower, however, as I was about to soap myself up, I noticed a barely visible straight hairline pattern on my soap's surface. Never having noticed this before, I carefully started digging with my fingernails and to my amazement discovered pieces of Gillette razor blades imbedded in the soap bar. Someone had done this in order to seriously injure me. Dr. Monroe, the state secretary of the Disciples' Ohio churches, a kind and very talented educator, was terribly upset when I reported this to him. He managed to find out who the culprit was and why the boy had done it. The confessed reason: "Mr. Ziffer is a Jew and the Jews killed our savior Jesus. It was only right to punish this Jew." The boy was expelled from Camp Christian. His parents, who came to pick him up, apologized. They confessed being deeply shocked by their son's action.

How could this have happened, I asked myself. Surely, the boy must have acquired this kind of hatred from someone else. Who might this someone else have been if not parents, family members, teachers or preachers? Might not I, by becoming a Christian minister and teacher, be an influence for good by teaching the Christian virtue of love – even for Jews?

CHAPTER 15
# Gibsonburg, Ohio and Graduate School of Theology

It was with a small heartache that I resigned my position with the Inland Division in Dayton. When I assured Mr. O'Brien, the division manager, a short potbellied Irish man, that my resignation was not revocable by means of a salary raise which he said he would gladly consider, he inquired how he could help with our resettlement and entry into my new chosen profession of a minister. This was a truly noble and welcome offer. I asked if he could provide me with a wide-carriage typewriter to facilitate my typing of stencils for the printing of the church worship service bulletins. My request did not fall on deaf ears. Shortly after our arrival in Gibsonburg, a small town south of Toledo, Ohio, where I was to begin a student ministry at the Garfield Memorial Church of Christ, a GM salesman on the way to Detroit dropped off just such a machine. Why Gibsonburg? Because this town's Church of Christ happened to have an opening for a theology student as their pastor, and it was located about seventy miles west of Oberlin.

The small congregation welcomed our family warmly. The basement of the white clapboard church building with its short bell tower extension was filled with smiling women and men standing around tables heaped with full sacks of groceries. This is truly an auspicious beginning to my ministry, I thought.

*Confronting the Silence*

But things aren't always as sweet as they look. The parsonage was an old building without storm windows. When the wind and snow blew outside, a frequent happening in that part of the country, it blew right into our rooms. The basement, where on my Roneo machine I printed the service bulletins, flooded quite often. The floors creaked. This was not a good place to bring up little children. Now we had three girls: Ruth Campbell a toddler, Deborah Ann a preschooler, and Elizabeth Zell entering first grade. Our son, Timothy Leo, would be born in nearby Fremont, Ohio, and his health was precarious at first. Most of the G-burg men worked in the town's large gypsum quarry. And when, after the first rain, we wondered about the white streaky deposits on the cars that were parked on the street, we were told it was gypsum in the air that was washed down by the rain. The deaths of many of the folks I buried there during my four-year pastorate were cancer-related.

Ministry for me and for Carolyn was difficult. For the first two years of my studies at Oberlin, there was the daily hour-and-a-half drive to school and then back home. During our time in northern Ohio (Sandusky County), I came down three times with flu and once with viral pneumonia that necessitated hospitalization at the Fremont hospital. We knew this regime could not go on any longer. During the third and fourth years, I arranged my courses so I could stay near campus in a rented room four days of the week. I returned home for a long weekend of church work and study. This arrangement was somewhat more viable. However, while my own workload and travel became increasingly taxing on my physical and mental health, Carolyn's caring for four young children without my help turned out to be very difficult as well. And there were other problems.

The two elders and spiritual leaders of the church were fundamentalists who met in closeted meetings with a couple of elderly women who every so often appeared out of nowhere to study the Bible. The result of these sessions came to light when, in these two men's prayers

## Gibsonburg, Ohio and Graduate School of Theology

introducing the weekly communion service, they tried to contradict much that I had taught in the preceding sermon. Oberlin's Graduate School of Theology (GST) was a theologically liberal school where critical methodology in the study of texts was taught and applied. This clashed with these men's bent for a literal and often far-fetched mystical interpretation of texts. Needless to say, neither one of the two elders had even a smattering of Hebrew or Greek. Frustrating as this regular Sunday morning interference with my efforts at teaching was, I kept on sharing with my congregation as best I could the exciting new insights into the scriptures I was receiving at school.

Shortly after our arrival in Gibsonburg, Mr. B., one of these church elders took me on an exploration of the little town. Not seeing a single person of color in the streets surprised me. I voiced this surprise while we stood at the closed railroad crossing waiting for the train to pass. "Good question," he responded. "Let me explain. Years ago I stood at this very place and saw a nigger with a bundle over his shoulder walking down the tracks. He stopped and wanted to know things about our town. I cut him short and said to him, 'No need to talk, boy. Just keep on walking.'" With a twinkle in his eyes, Mr. B. then added, "You sure understand, Reverend, don't you?" This little exchange did nothing to advance our friendship.

Every summer, migrant workers from Mexico came to our town for the harvest. It was good to see some of our church women helping the families, delivering used clothes, toys and personal hygiene items. I sometimes took the family along to the miserable encampments where some of the housing was barely converted chicken coops. I offered assistance and tried to make the families feel welcome. A young Spanish-speaking college student also arrived, sent by a church organization, to help with the migrant children's entertainment and education. I remember her sitting on the hood of her car, teaching the little ones around her the Spanish church song, *"Yo tengo un amigo que me ama...."*

On one such occasion, their leader, Mr. Gonzalez, an elderly man with a deeply wrinkled face, asked whether they could attend our church. My answer was, of course, affirmative. On second thought I wondered how my two elders, both not well-disposed toward people of color, would handle the serving of communion to these poor, dark-faced migrants. Things went better than I thought. One Sunday they all came to church, filling half the empty pews. Communion time arrived. I noticed a look of revulsion on Mr. B.'s face as he handed to one of the men, sitting at the end of the front pew, the tray with bread and the platter with the small containers of grape juice to be passed on down the line. In all honesty, the sour expression on his face gave me much satisfaction. Afterwards, Mr. B. reprimanded me with, "Reverend, you should have consulted with us elders. Surely you know these migrants are Catholic. Why not send them to their own church?"

Another memory is of Mrs. H., our organist and daughter of one of the two elders. After some sermons of which she probably disapproved, she would ask me in a sweet voice, "Reverend, are you sure you're still not a Jew? This sermon, you know, did not sound very Christian to me." I learned how to politely laugh this off, and it wasn't too hard since, in addition to assisting me with the music, she regularly treated our whole family to a delicious Sunday dinner where the children played with puppies in the barn or viewed their first Shirley Temple movie on Mr. B.'s television set. More happily for me, most people did not challenge me, offering only their trust, such as elderly Mrs. R. who asked me if it was a sin to ask God to let her physically handicapped and retarded sixty-year-old daughter die before her, because no one else could take care of Honey if Mrs. R. passed away first. With other parishioners there was camaraderie, as with good ol' Pete who tried to make me laugh during my sermon by ostentatiously combing himself with a foot-long comb. We went fishing together on Lake Erie. The next Sunday, as we snacked together in the fellowship hall after the service, Pete stood up and announced he had something important to share with the congregation. He then recounted how the Reverend (that is I) got seasick in the boat and "fed the fish." Pete's reward for the story was hilarious laughter and well-meaning thunderous applause.

On a more serious note, let me say that my relationship to Christianity was utterly genuine. For twenty-two years I faithfully served the Christian church, both as pastor and as seminary professor. My fidelity to the faith was never questioned by anyone. Yet I must confess that I felt uncomfortable with the Christian dogmas of the incarnation and the trinity. I very much admired and continue to admire the person of Jesus, *Yeshua ha-Notzriy* (Jesus of Nazareth) as he was called in his lifetime: a wise faithful and loving Jewish person, desperately trying to reform his own religion. But considering him to have been God incarnate was too much of a non-intellectual leap for me.

My protracted absences from home damaged the relationship between Carolyn and me. Marriage, even the best of marriages which I considered ours to be, is a fragile bond. Despite Carolyn's initial enthusiastic approval of our choice to go into the Christian ministry, neither one of us had realized the difficulties this chosen path would create for both of us. On Carolyn's side of the relationship, the demands of bringing up four little children without a proper husband to be there and to help were enormous. Without doubt I underestimated the severe hardship she suffered as the result of my absentee fatherhood. But even had I fully understood her misery, what could I have done, short of dropping our future plans altogether?

While I dearly loved and missed my wife and my children, my forced absence was compensated by exhilaration about my field of study and satisfaction that my life's goal was coming ever closer into view. Important byproducts of this gratification were new friendships with like-minded people.

Professor Herbert Gordon May, teaching Old Testament and biblical Hebrew, was my favorite teacher. Under his tutelage I learned exegesis of biblical texts. In my third year of study I had advanced sufficiently to work with him on a translation of the so-called "Community Rule," one of the relatively well-preserved and important texts of the Dead Sea Scrolls from Qumran. Dr. May, a premier archaeologist who excavated at Megiddo with the Oriental Institute of the University of Chicago, became my role model. The relationship went further when he invited me to accompany him for several weeks on a trip through the Middle East (Egypt, Jordan, Israel, Lebanon and Syria) to visit archaeological sites in connection with his editorship of the *Oxford Bible Atlas*. What I learned from Herb May is truly inestimable, and my gratitude for his scholarship and friendship defies description. To this day I remember with grief his last visit with us in Brussels, Belgium, shortly after which a common friend informed me that he had committed suicide.

Several of my fellow students enjoyed studying with me. As a Jewish youngster I learned to read Hebrew fairly fluently without necessarily understanding what I was reading. For many non-Jewish theology students, just mastering the Hebrew alphabet is difficult, so my help was welcome. One such student was Marie, a pretty young woman from South Dakota, also studying theology at the GST. We became friends, studying together, and being away from my wife for days at a time, there were temptations. Carolyn, in her physical isolation, expressed frustration at my seeming need when at home only "to have your laundry done and to have sex." The words hurt deeply and did nothing to strengthen our married relationship. After graduation from GST with two Master degrees, one in Old Testament studies and one in New Testament and Greek, and our subsequent assignment to a position in France, Marie disappeared from my life. What I learned from this sweet and potentially destructive episode was that even a healthy marriage is vulnerable under certain circumstances. Physical proximity of marriage partners, which includes sexual activity, strengthens the bonds of love.

My studies at GST were a life-changing experience. While the theological orientation of the school was generally liberal, the issues dealing with Jewish-Christian relations were pretty much ignored by all the teachers. Dick Wolf, our Church History professor, a staunch Lutheran, a good pedagogue and a fine scholar or so it seemed to me, rather cavalierly dismissed the medieval Crusades, the Inquisition, the Blood Libel and the Black Death, and how these impacted Jewish communities in a deadly way. As I play all this back in my mind, it seems to me that in my admiration of Dr. Wolf I was oblivious to his shortcomings in this respect. My eyes were opened toward the end of a Martin Luther course when, doing research for a paper, I consulted the library's German Weimar edition of Luther's works. Sitting on the library ladder and perusing one of these volumes, I discovered two works which Professor Wolf had never even mentioned. One was a treatise entitled *That Jesus Christ Was Born a Jew* (1523), and a later one was titled *On the Jews and Their Lies* (1543). In the first, Luther condemns the inhuman treatment of the Jews and urges Christians to treat them kindly. He expresses his fervent wish that Jews would hear the gospel and be moved to convert to Christianity. When this wish was not fulfilled as he had hoped, Luther's attitude toward the Jews changed drastically. The second treatise is rabidly antisemitic, going so far as to recommend that synagogues be burnt down, that the rabbis be forbidden to preach, and that other steps be taken by Christians against the Jews, who are "full of the devil's feces…which they wallow in like swine." Luther calls the synagogue an "incorrigible whore and an evil slut."

When I asked Dr. Wolf the next morning in class why he had never mentioned this not-so-admirable writing of his hero Luther, there was an embarrassed silence followed by, "This is the work of an old Luther who undoubtedly began suffering from senility. I felt it unnecessary to deal with these texts." To me the response was inadequate, to say the least, and I lost respect for Dick Wolf. But I did wonder what the real reason was for Wolf's silence on this subject.

Two weeks or so prior to graduation, we were interviewed by prospective employers. One of these was a man from New York, representing the United Church (of Christ) Board for World Ministries (UCBWM). The organization had openings in Micronesia and in Suva on Fiji. I knew that Carolyn would reject both out of hand. Just before leaving, the good man said, "Well, there is also a post in France that is available, but to fill that vacancy we need someone who speaks French." This, I knew, was for us. I spoke French. We accepted the offer and arrived in Le Chambon-sur-Lignon (Haute Loire) on July 4, 1964, American Independence Day.

CHAPTER 16
# Le Chambon and Montpellier, France

Before embarking for France, we spent a few weeks down on the Kinnard farm in Franklin. The children always enjoyed their stay at the grandparents' beautiful homestead. There were kittens to play with, and there was fishing. For both Carolyn and me, this vacation was a chance to brush up on our French. Looking back, these days were our last ones together with my mother-in-law, who was starting a terminal battle with colon cancer. The separation of Carolyn and her mother would be harder on her than I then realized.

*Accueil Fraternel* or "Brotherly Welcome" was a conference center in Le Chambon-sur-Lignon, located in south central France on a three thousand foot high plateau with at least two partially eroded volcanoes. The snow and ice in late fall and winter were rather uninviting. When spring and summer arrived, the fields, dotted with boulders, broke out into carpets of daffodils. Our destination in this small town was a remodeled stone farm house with an adjacent small chapel (itself a converted low barn). A wooden chalet-style conference wing and an additional small house at the entrance to the property completed this mini-campus which, after the war, had been established to facilitate reconciliation between French and German intellectuals who might hasten understanding between Protestants of two former enemy nations. The Center was also used as a sort of inn for parents of middle and high-school boarders at the *Collège Cévenol*, a private secondary school whose orientation was education for peace. Howard Schomer, an American clergyman interested in pacifism and peacemaking, had become a teacher at the *Collège* and had founded the *Accueil Fraternel* with the financial help of the United Church of Christ (UCC) denomination, of which he was a member.

By 1964, when I accepted the directorship of the Center, its peacemaking-related mission had ceased. The previous director, also an American, had left, and the UCC in conjunction with the Reformed Church of France was seeking a new orientation for the *Accueil*. This is where I came in. "Find a new orientation for the Center, but do not get involved in the politics of the *Collège Cévenol*," which at that particular time was in the throes of discord and turmoil about issues linked to the succession of its director.

In a predominantly Roman Catholic country, the population of Le Chambon-sur-Lignon and its immediate vicinity was almost totally Protestant with theological roots in Calvinism. Almost all people here belonged to the *Eglise Reformée de France*, which emerged from the Reformation of the sixteenth century, their ancestors being the savagely persecuted Huguenots. What I did not know as we set out for our ministry in France was that the good people of Le Chambon, during World War II, had saved approximately 3,500 Jewish refugees fleeing Hitler's persecution by hiding them – and in so doing risked their own lives. Books have been written and videos produced about the heroism of the *Chambonnais*: the people of the little town and their pastor André Trocmé and his wife Magda who inspired their flock's heroic actions. Today a large plaque affixed to the church wall witnesses to the gratitude of the Jews who survived thanks to the town people's courage. At *Yad Vashem*, the Jerusalem Holocaust Authority's "Avenue of the Righteous Among the Nations," a tree and a plaque beneath it bear witness to pastor André and Magda Trocmé's role in

## Le Chambon and Montpellier, France

the saving of Jewish lives.

Shortly after accepting the position at *Accueil*, I exchanged letters with the Center's secretary, Mademoiselle Germaine Rivet. Judging from our correspondence, I felt optimistic and reassured about our imminent mission in France. In one of the preparatory notes Germaine sent, I learned that upon arrival I would find at the Center a group of young people belonging to a German-wide Christian youth organization called *Der Offene Abend* (The Open Evening) from the city of Stuttgart. Now let's remember that the year was 1964, a rather significant date for me in that it was the same year that I read Elie Wiesel's book *Night*, his Auschwitz memoir, in English. As I read it, memories of my Holocaust-related experiences, very similar to the author's, flooded back. The news that I would be encountering young Germans for the first time after my liberation from the Nazi camps became a real worry to me. What if they extended their hand to greet me; would I – could I – be able to accept that hand and grip it? In all probability some of these youngsters' parents, still alive, had murdered Jews. Despite my conversion to Christianity, the Jewish people had remained my people! How I would manage this imminent face-to-face meeting remained a serious apprehension for me.

As it turned out, my worry was unfounded. These were friendly and open-minded young people with whom I was able to shake hands. On several occasions I accepted their invitation to participate in their New Testament study, and I remember sharing with them my theological insights which they genuinely appreciated. Upon departure for home in Germany, they presented me with an illustrated modern version of the New Testament in German.

I do not remember anymore exactly how Carolyn and I happened upon the idea of transforming the now defunct conference center into a language center for non-French missionaries and development workers whose destinations were certain West African nations. Because of these countries' past colonial connections to France, the vehicular language among the many peoples there, who speak different dialects and languages and cannot communicate with one another often from village to village, has remained French. I faintly recall that a language center in Paris used by churches was no longer considered effective. The complaint was that their students, non-French missionaries headed to Africa, tended to continue speaking their native languages among themselves, which kept them from acquiring adequate communication skills in French. Also, the many cultural diversions of Paris seemed counterproductive to concentration on language study. What we could offer in Le Chambon, on the other hand, was a total immersion experience in French language study.

When I communicated our proposal to my bosses at the UCBWM in New York, I immediately received a green light to proceed. This resulted in an extended trip that took me to churches and mission societies in Denmark, Norway, Sweden, Germany, Holland and Belgium. I was well received, and on occasion, as it happened in Stavanger, Norway, informally examined over dinner with regard to my theological orientation. Shortly after my return to France, the future missionaries began trickling, then streaming in, not only from the countries I had visited but also from the U.S., Canada, England, Switzerland and Finland. This success, which was not without accompanying headaches, called for expansion of our facilities. That problem was solved by a generous gift of a large pre-fab building donated to us by the World Council of Churches in Geneva. Toward the end of my five-year tenure as director, our center housed around sixty adults and children taught by a small staff of local educators. The *Accueil Fraternel* venture was a success. It gave Carolyn and me satisfaction that we had achieved the task entrusted to us, and that the language-school orientation of *Accueil* turned out to be a necessary and useful tool for furtherance of Christian world mission.

I was pleased to find in one of the two local pastors a very competent Hebraist. Once a week we studied Old Testament texts

## Le Chambon and Montpellier, France

together. *Monsieur le pasteur* André Lelièvre also happened to be an excellent preacher. When my secretary Germaine, who sat on the church council, once confided to me that she had heard Lelièvre say that he considered Ziffer to be a good preacher, I was thrilled. It was in Le Chambon that I began considering studies toward a doctorate of theology. Of the three theological faculties available, I chose the Protestant faculty of the University of Strasbourg, this being the only state university offering such a program. Upon graduation from the GST at Oberlin summa cum laude, the school had granted me a one-thousand dollar scholarship toward doctoral study. My mentor Herbert G. May approved of my choice and promised to recommend me to his old friend *Professeur* Edmond Jacob, a prominent European Old Testament scholar who subsequently became my dissertation advisor at Strasbourg. As director of *Accueil Fraternel* in Le Chambon, a virtual high place for French Protestants, and thanks to some published work of mine appearing in the Protestant press, I became known in French Protestant circles as a competent American Old Testament scholar. Daniel Lys, the titular Old Testament professor at the *Faculté de Théologie Protestante* in Montpellier, France, took notice. Toward the end of my tenure in Le Chambon, which could have been extended, Lys invited me to teach at the Montpellier seminary as a guest lecturer. The year was 1969. Carolyn and I accepted, and we moved to Montpellier, a beautiful city located about five miles from the Mediterranean coast.

I count the following three years there among my best. It was a thrill teaching at the seminary and associating formally as well as informally with some of the best European scholars. The students liked me and considered my teaching to be a fresh breeze in their stilted and, in their opinion, stale education. I felt highly honored when the faculty chose me to give *La Leçon d'ouverture* or the opening lecture of a new scholastic year in 1971 with the prefect of the department (Hérault) sitting in full regalia in the front row and applauding.

This was also the year I was accorded a doctorate in theology by the University of Strasbourg.

Life in Montpellier was good and enjoyable. Carolyn could now relax without having to worry what to serve all those missionaries with their disparate tastes, only at times to be criticized afterwards. She was able to be a full-time parent to our four children. All four kids did well in their respective schools. Mediterranean beaches were close by, and we enjoyed them. My students became our friends. Carolyn and I purchased an old *mas* (traditional farmhouse), a part of an abandoned farm in the hills north of the city, for our vacation times. Surrounded by vineyards, in the vicinity of a small stream, in the shadow of the ruin of the castle of Fressac up a steep hill, we spent weekends and vacations. Being somewhat of a handyman, I made improvements to the property to make it more "vacationable." I remember pleasant evenings around a campfire with some of my students playing the guitar and singing and afterwards indulging in a meal of roasted rabbit.

I owe a tremendous debt to Professor May who often told me, "Just call me Herb," something I could not do even after I had become a doctor of theology myself and we had attended a number of theological conferences together. The conference organized by the International Organization for the Study of the Old Testament, held in Rome at the Vatican, stands out for me from those in Geneva, Switzerland, and Göttingen, Germany. There, I believe, I found and appropriated for myself the personal mission I was to engage in from then on. Augustin Cardinal Bea, head of the Vatican Secretariat for Jewish-Christian Relations, a red-hatted, physically miniscule person but a theological giant, hosted the reception. Dr. May introduced me to him, mentioning my Holocaust experience and interest in Jewish-Christian dialogue. With our champagne glasses in hand, the cardinal took me by the arm and led me away from the scholars' chatter. This is what he then said to me: "Young man, Jewish-Christian dialogue will not succeed in reaching its goal of spiritual unity until the Jews dig down to the bedrock of their faith, and until the Christians dig down to the bedrock of their faith. Having done so, they will find themselves standing on the same rock. Only then will they realize that they are brothers and sisters." It is these words that have guided me in my work ever since that memorable day in Rome. I wish I had asked the cardinal what he meant by "bedrock," but I was too intimidated to do so. It would be interesting to know whether his "bedrock" metaphor referred to ethical behavior, something perhaps like Rabbi Hillel's "Do not do to others what is hateful to you," or the words of Jesus that rephrase Hillel's teaching: "Do unto others what you would have them do unto you," often called the Golden Rule.

I consider the three years of my teaching ministry in Montpellier among the highlights of my Christian ministry experience. On a more mundane level, I enjoy remembering our Saint-Clément apartment's marble-like floors, the balconies looking out over the gardens below, the sheer curtains that moved gently with the breeze from the sea nearby, and most of all the friendships with my learned colleagues from whom I never heard an anti-Jewish word. We could have stayed on in Montpellier. But our children had become culturally and linguistically French, and Carolyn feared they would lose their American heritage altogether. She felt the time had come to return home. And so we did. Our new destination was Washington, DC.

## CHAPTER 17
# Washington, DC

The United Church of Christ's ministerial placement service in New York City helped me procure the pastorate of the Concordia UCC, one of the oldest Washington congregations, located in the Foggy Bottom neighborhood of the District of Columbia. Housed in a white-washed neo-gothic brick building with a non-functioning bell tower, Concordia had been founded by German immigrants. The church wanted to offer German services in addition to the regular English ones, so my native German language was an asset that made them invite me to be their pastor.

After nine years in France, personal and professional reintegration into the American scene was not easy. Elizabeth, our oldest, had remained in Montpellier to obtain her French baccalaureate (one year more advanced than a high school diploma). It was with a heavy heart that we said goodbye to her for a year. Deborah, Ruth and Tim began their American educational adventure with some trepidation, but they succeeded thanks to Carolyn's total involvement in their adjustment to the American system.

My ministry with Concordia went generally well, but there were run-ins with those members of the congregation who worked for the government. This was the time of the Vietnam War and the

*Confronting the Silence*

Watergate scandal. The president of the congregation happened to be the librarian of the CIA library, and her husband was in charge of CIA recruitment of technical personnel. Both reacted quite strongly to my anti-Vietnam and anti-Nixon preaching. At times these two and other government employees stood up and walked out on me. I shrugged this off as inevitable and kept on doing what seemed only right and necessary to me.

What did bother me, however, were incidents of antisemitism. None of these was ever directed openly against my person as a convert from Judaism. Let me relate here just two such incidents that upset me. On Sunday afternoons I would take communion to my shut-in parishioners who lived all over the city, mostly elderly folks. In the case of one lady of German background, she excused herself prior to our brief prayers and went to her bedroom, leaving the door open behind her. Glancing in, I saw a crucifix hanging above the headboard of the bed. This aroused my curiosity, because the equivalent symbol for Protestants is a simple unadorned cross. A crucifix is usually associated with Roman Catholic worship. When she returned to the living room, I asked her why the crucifix. A lengthy but evasive conversation ensued. In the end she told me how, during the war, on her way to her job in a munitions factory, she passed by a pawnshop window where she spotted this crucifix lying among other objects, for sale. She felt she had to purchase it. Too shy to enter to find out how much it cost, she sent a friend. The price was $5.00, she was told. Now she began assiduously saving pennies from her meager wages until she finally arrived at $3.50. She mustered her courage, entered the shop, and told the owner of her great desire to purchase the crucifix. She asked him if he would let her have the cross for the $3.50 which she had arduously set aside. She promised to pay the balance at a later time. To her joy, the shopkeeper not only gave her the coveted crucifix, but forgave her the $1.50 she owed. She was overjoyed, and she had this crucifix attached to the wall above the headboard of her bed. I was deeply touched by the story, but wanted to know more. "Why were you so determined to purchase this particular crucifix?" I asked. "After all, you are a Protestant, and Protestants use a simple cross instead of one with the Christ nailed to it." "Reverend," she answered, "I just could not stand seeing our crucified Savior lying in the window of a Jew-shop." That was almost more than I could take. I did not respond, gave her communion, and rushed out.

Another example of antisemitism took place after a Sunday service, when I had preached a sermon dealing with what I called "the sin of antisemitism." After the last congregant had thanked me and left by the front door, two elders of the church came up to me. "Reverend, we want to tell you something." What followed was an antisemitic joke. What kind of people are these, I wondered.

While in DC, I was invited to join the faculty of Inter-faith Metropolitan Education, Inc., generally known as Inter/Met theological seminary, and I accepted. Teaching in this newly formed institution with its multinational and multiracial student body provided me with the intellectual stimulation that the church did not provide, especially since the church membership consisted predominantly of tradition-oriented persons of moderate education.

Two nearby downtown churches, one United Methodist and the other United Presbyterian, suffered just as we did from the exodus of downtown dwellers to suburbia, with only the older and most faithful members continuing to commute to our locations downtown for Sunday services and special events. All three of our churches' financial situations were grim, and the hope to enlarge our respective congregations was dim. Being on friendly terms with the Presbyterian minister, we often discussed our dilemma. He suggested the idea of a possible merger of the three struggling groups. Eventually the Methodist minister joined us, and the three congregations entered into exploratory talks about the feasibility of such a move. Many meetings and months later, the project came to a vote. To my disappointment, the Presbyterians who had initiated the idea of the merger opted out. Rather than ditching the project at that point, the United Methodist and our UCC congregations went ahead and merged, with the agreement that their pastor and I would become co-pastors of the newly born United Church – a church functioning to this day.

What followed was nothing less than tragic. With the Methodist minister's theological orientation being fundamentalist and mine being liberal, the newly formed "united" congregation divided along these two positions, each one of us having a following. Both groups looked to their respective denominational ecclesiological backing which, in the case of the Methodists, was hierarchical with superintendents and bishops, and in our case congregational and democratic. It came to repeated clashes within our congregation and on the denominational level. The struggle for supremacy became uglier and uglier. In one congregational meeting I suggested a solution to end the strife: if the Methodist bishop were to transfer my Methodist co-pastor, I would resign my co-pastor's post. Visibly relieved, the church council and the denominational higher-ups accepted my proposed solution.

Our family was now without income. None of my job applications had panned out with the exception of one, still under consideration, with a church in Arlington, Virginia. The income from my teaching at Inter/Met was not sufficient for us to make ends meet. Our family was changing fast, with three girls in different east coast colleges and soon each one involved with a fiancé or boyfriend that would string our family out from DC and Philadelphia to Beersheva, Israel, and Beirut, Lebanon. Tim was still with us and in high school in Washington. Carolyn went to work at the jewelry counter of a nearby Sears store and hated every minute of it. Despite the hardship my decision had dumped on us, I did not regret having made it.

CHAPTER 18
# Brussels, Belgium

Desperate to find employment, I turned to the UCBWM for help. They told me I had just missed the deadline for applying to the American Protestant Church (APC) of Brussels, Belgium, which was looking for a pastor. Their advice: why not apply there anyway, since I had served in France, spoke French fluently, and therefore was eminently qualified for the position? And if that did not bring results, their office would keep me on file for future overseas openings.

I did just that, and what happened sounds like a small miracle. Mr. S., a member of the APC search committee and future friend, told me that my job application arrived after the committee had already drafted a letter of invitation to the chosen candidate. A sample sermon of mine, recorded on a cassette, was included with my letter. Despite this material being late, someone suggested they listen to the sermon. Everybody liked the sermon, but showed no intention of changing their mind. Wanting to hear the sermon again, Mr. S. took the cassette home and replayed it. Strangely, what he heard this time was not a sermon but my conversation with our children. He had inserted the wrong side of the cassette into the machine. On that side I was playing a recording by the German composer Max Bruch for my children. *Kol nidrei* is the chanted introductory Hebrew prayer to the Jewish high holy day worship service called the Day of Atonement, or *Yom Kippur* in Hebrew. What Mr. S. heard was my attempt to explain how the brilliant musician interpreted this prayer for God's forgiveness. The tape contained the children's questions and my answers. Mr. S. was so moved by what he heard that he called his colleagues on the search committee and suggested they halt their decision. They should all listen to the cassette tape first. They did, and the intended invitational letter was redirected to me. I became the pastor of the American Protestant Church of Brussels. The year was 1977.

Brussels is a cosmopolitan metropolis, and APC's congregation with its extensive English-speaking expatriate membership was a representative slice of the city. Presidents and vice-presidents of transnational corporations like Kraft Food and Exxon sat next to refugees from Ethiopia; ambassadors to NATO and high-ranking NATO officers sat next to African students from Leuven University, one of the oldest in Europe. There was a mix of denominations from Baptists and high church Lutherans to Methodists and Mennonites. Every Sunday the church was packed full, and on special religious holidays like Palm Sunday with confirmation services and baptisms, or Easter with its early Sunrise Service and later regular celebration, we could barely seat the overflow of congregants and visitors. They sat on stairs, on the floor, on sofas brought in from the offices, and many had to stand. For a pastor this was a dream come true. There were other English-speaking churches in Brussels: a Baptist church, an Episcopal cathedral, even a small Church of Scotland. Despite this variety, there was no competition. The various ministers and priests formed a friendly group.

Our spacious parsonage apartment easily accommodated our guests at the twice monthly teas Carolyn and I hosted. Our son Tim was still with us, attending the twelfth grade at the International School of Brussels on whose campus APC was located.

## Brussels, Belgium

Most of our congregants were highly educated. Thanks to one British-Belgian couple, ex-missionaries in the Congo, our church's interest and involvement in overseas mission were strong, with half our budget supporting medical Christian missions in Africa. Thanks to the intellectual interests and financial resources of our people, I organized a number of study trips to Israel and Egypt, which remain unforgettable.

Another highlight of the Belgian ministry was being invited to an international conference on biblical ethics under the aegis of the British Crown at Windsor Castle. The meetings took place in the castle library which, we were told, saw the first performance of Shakespeare's *Merry Wives of Windsor*, under its author's direction. Among the presenters was Lord Longford, keynote speaker for the occasion. Longford was a socialist member of the House of Lords, well-known for his liberal political outlook and advocacy for good Christian relations with the country's Jews. In the Lord's keynote address, he suggested that Christian ethics based on Jesus' New Testament teachings superseded rabbinic teaching because of its ethical superiority. According to Longford, even the well-known Oxford scholar Geza Vermes, a Christian with Jewish roots, had emphasized this in his writings. Pretty secure in my theological knowledge in both the Jewish and Christian traditions, and having read most of Vermes' theological output, I did not agree. I was certain that Longford's reading of Vermes was incorrect and that his thesis did not hold water. I became increasingly restless.

As soon as Lord Longford's speech came to an end and the Q&A session began, I, who in those days was something of a theological firebrand, jumped to my feet and told him that I respectfully disagreed with him. Rattling off a number of Talmudic ethical statements and adding that nowhere in the readings of Vermes had I ever found statements that Longford attributed to him, I admonished the Lord to rethink his thesis. There was silence in the large hall. Lord Longford was visibly shaken. Then came his response: "And you sir, tell me, where have you acquired such a *tendresse* for the Jewish people?" Now, the house exploded into laughter. Some laughed because they were aware of my Jewish background. But most of the laughter, I am certain, was due to the *faux pas* which the Lord had committed in inquiring about my *tendresse*, French for tenderness, for the Jews. With these words Longford betrayed his real feelings about the Jews, and revealed something akin to Christian superiority. Was Longford a hypocrite or even a covert antisemite?

There is a somewhat redeeming ending to this story. The Very Reverend Dr. Mann, Canon of Windsor Cathedral, came over to Carolyn and me sitting at breakfast the next morning. With a big grin on his face he said to me, "Dr. Ziffer, I have a message for you from Lord Longford. As I drove him to the train back to London, he asked me to express to you his apologies. 'Please say to the gentleman who took me to task after my lecture last night that I was both ignorant and arrogant and that I apologize.'" These humble and courageous words rehabilitated Lord Longford in my eyes, at least partially.

Why do I tell this incident in some detail? Because often in my life I have heard respectable and intelligent people, triggered by their uncontrolled fervor for an idea or issue, vent statements highly offensive to minorities like Jews or homosexuals, people physically or mentally challenged, political opponents, etc., which I would never have thought these folks capable of uttering. These are latent feelings that for "politically correct" reasons are suppressed, but which, at times of stress or extreme agitation, slip out and unmask the speaker's true attitudes.

This brings me to an unpleasant recollection from the time prior to my ordination to become a Christian minister. A few days before graduation from seminary, those of us who desired ordination by our respective denominations were required to meet with a group of clergy to be examined. Paul Miguel from Hawaii, a fellow Oberlin student, and I traveled in this connection to Cleveland to undergo this largely pro forma test of proficiency in our field. On our way back to Oberlin, Paul said to me, "Walter, at the meeting back in Cleveland, I heard something that upset me. Because it pertains to you, I would like to share it with you, if you promise not to get angry at me. You know that sometimes it is the messenger of the message rather than the message he carries who is blamed." I assured Paul I would not be angry with him regardless of what the information contained. "Walter, after I was dismissed by the clergy examiners, one of them asked, 'Who is next?' To which one of the examiners responded with, 'It is that Jew, Ziffer.'"

Upon return to the seminary I phoned Dr. Herald Monroe, the secretary of the Ohio Disciples of Christ churches in Cleveland, and lodged my complaint with him. His answer was curt and to the point. "Thanks for letting me know, Walter. You will hear more about this soon." Later that evening I received a call from the minister who had referred to me as "that Jew, Ziffer." The man expressed his regret and apologized. I accepted his apology, of course. All this is to say that it is impossible to know what thoughts and attitudes lodge deep within all of us. On occasions our secret emotions explode into overt offensive words and actions. This is when our true selves come to light.

Brussels, for me, was an exciting time of ministry. But alas, as I indicated in the preceding paragraphs, there loom in us hidden emotions and sentiments, often consciously suppressed, but often also unknown to ourselves. When triggered by certain exterior occurrences, these erupt out of their self-created protective shells where they have been lying dormant, and raise havoc with our and others' lives. Totally unexpected to me at the time, Carolyn came down with deep depression. Our life together had been harmonious to the best of my knowledge for over three decades. If there were indications of a gathering storm, I certainly was oblivious to this. It is not unusual, I am told, that in some cases of depression, self-hatred erupts as well as animosity against those living closest to the afflicted person. Our life in Europe and Carolyn's life as a minister's spouse had become an unbearable burden.

It is impossible to describe how difficult it is to live with a clinically depressed person under one roof. Unable to wrap my mind around my wife's sudden loss of love for me, I brooded constantly about what I may have done wrong to bring this about, but insight eluded me. Naturally I also mulled over possible approaches to improve the situation, and that also proved unsuccessful. In my foolishness, when all this started, I would beg her to "please *snap* out of this craziness." Big mistake! My beloved wife, usually calm and gentle, exploded into uncontrollable weeping upon hearing such words. Often, in the middle of the night, she would wake up and throw a temper tantrum. I see myself walking through the empty streets of Brussels in the darkness, kicking at the walls of houses and at tree trunks. Our sexual relationship became a thing of the past. Despite our living in close physical proximity, we became strangers. I found myself rejected, abandoned, totally alone. We had unending visits to psychologists and psychiatrists, all unsuccessful. I became afraid of my wife. I was paralyzed in my work. During my sermons I feared she would get up to contradict loudly what I was saying, or even call me a hypocrite in public. Fortunately, this never happened, but for sure our marriage was beginning to unravel. Yet in spite of the agony of that miserable time, I remember vividly two episodes where Carolyn rallied to calm my anxiety and diminish my acute physical pain, and still today, I remember those times with gratitude.

One evening, after a sunny afternoon when I sat on our balcony enjoying the rarity of a blue sky and sunshine in Brussels, a pleasant departure from the usual gray drizzly Brussels weather, I succeeded in coaxing Carolyn to come downtown with me to see a movie. While sitting in the theater and looking at the emergency exit signs, I wondered about the luminous halos around them. On our way back home on the tram, all the streetlights were surrounded by a halo. Without paying further attention to this strange phenomenon,

## Brussels, Belgium

we went to bed. The next morning I woke up and could not focus. Everything was just an amorphous mass before me. I was able to distinguish between light and dark, but that was about all. When I apprised Carolyn of my quasi-blindness, she sprang into action. We raced by taxi to the nearest clinic: no eye doctor on duty there. We raced on to the nearest hospital: no eye doctor there, either. So on to Saint-Luc University Hospital, far out by the airport, where an ophthalmologist arrived on short call. The diagnosis after a thorough examination suggested I had partially burned corneas caused by an interaction between a sunscreen lotion applied to my face and eyelids and the unusually intense sun that afternoon. The doctor applied pressure bandages with a medication to both eyes. He reassured us that healing would set in quickly, and advised us to return in two days. The physician was a young Peruvian, I remember.

Carolyn's behavior that morning was in stark contrast to previous weeks. I remember her expressing outrage in the strongest of terms to the various hospital employees who failed to help us. She commandeered taxi cab after taxi cab in search of an eye specialist. She was kind and helpful to me, who was unable to see. Despite my misery and fearfulness of perhaps never being able to see again, I hoped that her sudden change in behavior signaled the end of her depression.

Two days later at Saint-Luc's the young doctor removed my bandages. I cannot describe the trepidation I went through in the process. Had I or had I not regained my eyesight? When the last piece of bandage came off, I saw again. The Peruvian physician had made the correct diagnosis and applied the proper treatment. To my shame I now confess that when I heard the nationality of this doctor as being Peruvian – not Belgian, not European – I had felt quite anxious. Thoughts like "A doctor from a third world country? Do they have reliable medical schools there?, obviously smack of racial prejudice and feelings of American superiority. I do hope this episode with a happy ending cured me for good of such wrong attitudes.

An event rather similar to the one described above resulted in a temporary reprieve from Carolyn's illness. It happened during my bout with and subsequent surgery for an enlarged prostate, also in Brussels. In this case, too, her behavior took a complete turn for the better, and I thought that our misery had finally and definitively come to an end. Sadly, this was not the case. Before long, Carolyn's depressed state recurred.

As my term of employment with APC neared its end, we decided to leave Belgium. During my ministry in Washington we had acquired forty acres in Nova Scotia, one of Canada's Maritime Provinces. We already loved the place from tent camping trips there. Beaver Lake in Queens County, Nova Scotia, and its surrounding beautiful woods held memories of glorious vacation days of boating, fishing, campfires, fun and close family life. Eventually, with some of the proceeds from the sale of the farm in Franklin, which Carolyn and her brother inherited, we had a small house built in the midst of a three-acre clearing. My hope was that our geographic relocation, far from the hustle and bustle of the large European city and my demanding job, would help Carolyn recover her full mental health. And so at the age of fifty-five, considerably weakened from my recent surgery, I retired from active ministry. Our destination was the tiny village of Kempt, close to the small town of Caledonia, in the southern part of Nova Scotia. The year was 1982.

## CHAPTER 19
## Nova Scotia, Canada

Our retirement to Kempt in Nova Scotia was everything I hoped it would be. As landed residents in the country, Carolyn and I enjoyed the same privileges as any Canadians, especially the near-free medical care that, on one occasion, I was forced to use. The small house I had designed myself while in Brussels soon had to be enlarged to allow space for our studies. So the original single garage became a double his-and-her study with a large picture window. Onto it we attached a one-and-a-half car garage with a loft where Tim stayed until he left for St. Louis and his girlfriend Claire. Later the two married.

What more was there to wish for a nature-loving person than to live within 150 feet of a fifty-acre lake where he could boat and fish trout or bass whenever he so desired? Now I even had my dream of a large garden (forty by eighty feet) and a motorized tiller. Good neighbors, within a mile or two in both directions, were also a blessing. The forest land was home to deer, rabbit and black bear – a novice hunter's paradise. We lived off the land with minimal expenses. One of my greatest acquisitions while in Canada was a puppy whom we named Lyla, a setter and retriever mix with predominant black Labrador features. Lyla turned out to be an intelligent, highly trainable, loving dog that kept me faithful company walking through the woods, as well as sitting by the tub when I bathed. She gave me great joy for eleven years, and I loved her dearly.

My father introduced my older sister Edith and me to the German poet Friedrich Schiller's beautiful poems. In his poem "The Ring of Polycrates," the king of Samos receives the visit of the king of Egypt. When the former brags to his visitor about his successes and his unbounded happiness, Egypt's king warns him about the fickleness of fate. During this very conversation, messengers arrive who report about victories on the battlefield and about the king's fleet, loaded with spoil from a naval engagement, arriving safely in the harbor. Uneasy about all this luck, the king throws his signet ring into the ocean in order to appease the gods who, jealous of his luck, might retaliate with disaster. The next morning he is awakened by a fisherman who gives the king the present of the largest and most beautiful fish he ever caught. As the royal cook prepares the fish, he finds in its stomach the very signet ring the king threw into the ocean the previous day. For the royal visitor from Egypt, such luck is too much and surely spells imminent disaster. In haste he leaves his host. "I can no longer dwell with you. You can no longer be my friend. The Gods have destined you to perish, and I do not wish to die with you." The beautiful poem made a powerful impression on me as a youngster. There were times after the Holocaust when I feared that my good life would someday collapse and turn into a catastrophe.

And so it also happened. During a picnic outing with Carolyn in Kejimkujik National Park, I had pulled out my old portable typewriter and was typing away on a manuscript. The sky was blue, the birds chirped, and the right words were coming to me as we sat with the soothing sounds of wavelets from Kejdgi Lake lapping up against the shallow shore.

My mood was suddenly interrupted. "Quit humming so loud! I can't read because of you." Brief silence. Then, "Your banging on the typewriter irritates me. Can't you stop for a while? Give me a break!" I stopped typing. "Come on now, Carolyn," I responded. "You know that when an idea pops into one's head one must get it down on paper as quickly as possible. But, OK. I'll stop for a while." I left the table for a quick walk along the shore of the lake to air out my head, as it were. I remember the apprehension that suddenly invaded me. Could it be…? I returned to the table and resumed typing. Soon after, Carolyn kept lambasting me with complaints and accusations. I did not understand. I was in shock. After a number of attempts to find out what had gotten into her, I ended my stuttering with, "I love you." Hunched over on the bench, she looked up at me with eyes I had never seen before. There was hatred and revulsion in her look. Slowly, in a whisper, came from nearly white lips the words, "But I do not love you." We packed up in silence and drove home. A feeling of helplessness overcame me. The words of Schiller and my worst fear sprang to mind: my happiness had ended in catastrophe. From this point on, apprehension about the immediate future hung like a menacing cloud above me. What followed were too many bleak days and nights that refuse and defy recollection, let alone description – like a living nightmare.

A ray of hope came into my life when in 1985 I received an unexpected invitation from the First Congregational Church of Longmeadow, Massachusetts. They wanted me to speak at their commemoration of *Yom HaShoah*, Holocaust Memorial Day. The invitation was initiated by an American couple who had been congregants at the Brussels church. I accepted the double opportunity of being able to teach and visit with our old friends. I also thought that this USA interlude might be beneficial to Carolyn. Both my sermon and the following evening lecture dealt with antisemitism and the Christian Church. From later correspondence with my friends, I was shocked to hear that they were criticized for having facilitated my visit to the Longmeadow church.

What I did not know was that during both my sermon and the evening lecture, two local rabbis were in the audience. One of them was Dr. Herman Eliot Snyder, a rather prestigious personality. Mingling afterwards over refreshments in the church's social hall, Rabbi Snyder joined me and said, "Dr. Ziffer, I am confused after your lecture. What I mean is that had I given this lecture, I probably would have said something very similar. Are you a Jew, or a member of the 'fifth column' in the church, a subversive?" There was no time for a one-on-one discussion. When the lady congregant from Brussels noticed the seriousness of our conversation, she invited the rabbi to have breakfast with us all the next morning at her home.

During coffee the next morning, Dr. Snyder turned to me and said in Hebrew *"Nelekh,"* meaning, "Let's go." We excused ourselves to an adjoining room. There, Snyder asked a lot of questions dealing with my past life. He was an extremely attentive listener and often asked for clarification. After forty-five minutes of this intensive exchange, I thanked him for his interest, at which time he took both my hands into his and said to me with a smile, "Walter, it is time for you to come home." I understood what he meant. My encounter with Rabbi Dr. Snyder was a crucial moment in my life journey. Carolyn and I returned to Nova Scotia.

This encounter coincided in time with another developing interest of mine. Now that I was secluded, I had time for serious reflection about antisemitism and my personal experiences. I felt driven to examine where, how and why this abominable ideology came into being. The outcome of my research resulted in the writing and publication of my first book, *The Teaching of Disdain: An Examination of Christology and New Testament Attitudes Toward Jews*. With half the manuscript written, I inquired whether the Anti-Defamation League (ADL) of B'nai B'rith, in collaboration with the Roman Catholic Paulist Press, might be interested in its publication. I met with Rabbi Klenicki in New York who, in tandem with the Paulist press, headed up the publication of a series dealing with Jewish-Christian dialogue. At the end of our meeting, I remember him saying, "Please send me the manuscript yesterday."

Once the completed manuscript was sent to him, a long waiting game ensued. I received a phone call from the new editor of the Paulist Press, a certain Father Boadt. He and the manuscript readers found the book interesting, but before they could consider publication, much of its content would have to be modified. His sense was that rather than bringing Jews and Christians together, which I hoped would result from the book, in his opinion it would provoke Christian alienation. Boadt suggested that I work with a Catholic priest-theologian to alter the text here and there so as to make it more palatable to a Christian readership. Convinced that such an approach would make major arguments fall through the cracks, I politely responded with, "Thank you, but no thank you." My daughter-in-law Claire worked at that time for a printing firm in Milwaukee that agreed to publish my book. Of course, without the advertising that the Paulist Press and ADL would have engaged in, the book sold half the number that it might have.

Now a word about the book's content. This work examined Jesus-related textual exegesis of the New Testament and linguistic matters. The main thesis of the book suggests that Jesus' death was a political expedient, used both by Rome and the Jewish Jerusalem hierarchy. While I cannot go into details here, let me just say that frequently the results I arrived at by applying Ockham's Razor (keep it simple) to certain complex biblical texts are not those easily accepted by the academic community; doing so would deprive scholars of further speculation and the publication of learned articles. When I sent a copy to Professor Daniel Lys, a biblical scholar and old friend from my days at the Montpellier seminary, he responded with thanks in a cool note implying that I had written the book out of anger as a Jew and Holocaust victim. Sadly, this brought our friendship to an end. Interestingly, on the other hand, many of my conclusions became accepted in the academic sphere as matters of fact within the next two decades.

*Confronting the Silence*

Our relatively isolated life in Nova Scotia, that I considered paradise at first, had turned into misery for both Carolyn and me. We decided to return to the United States. The question we pondered was, "Where?" For some reason Carolyn was fixed on Bangor, Maine. Every time we drove through Bangor on our way to camping in Nova Scotia, she used to say, "I feel we will someday live here and you will be teaching in Bangor." And so we moved and settled into the small town of Orrington, Maine, adjacent to the twin cities of Bangor-Brewer. The date was 1987.

CHAPTER 20
# Return to the USA: Bangor, Maine, and Weaverville, North Carolina

Maine is a beautiful state. The twin cities of Bangor-Brewer would be rather dull localities were it not for the impressive Penobscot River that separates them and brings to the area a measure of majesty. Orrington is a small New England village close by. We lived there in an old house that had been a store elsewhere and had been transported to its present location and set on a foundation. I refuse to go into detail about the troubles the basement caused us, especially during springtime with the huge accumulations of snow melting and water pouring in. Repairs consisted of enlarging sump holes and purchasing a reliable pump system. This cost us a lot of money and kept me awake many a night. Would we flood this time? My woodshop and the sleeping place for our dog Lyla were located down there.

We were not complete strangers to the area. We had come down from Nova Scotia a few years earlier and had spent three months at Bangor Theological Seminary, affiliated with the United Church of Christ. I was invited to fill the post of the school's Old Testament professor during his sabbatical in Europe. It was a good experience, marred only by the negative reaction of some faculty members when I suggested in a public lecture that antisemitism has been partially the result of certain Christian Church Fathers' misappropriation of New Testament texts and their radical anti-Jewish propaganda via sermons and writings during the second to seventh centuries. This time, however, having moved to Bangor for good, I was invited to teach in the Honors System of the University of Maine in nearby Orono, the flagship campus of the state-wide university system.

My first book was complete and had brought new religious insights to my life. My experiences of antisemitism as a Christian pastor, albeit never directed against my person but against the Jewish people, showed me that my theological and historical research had yielded correct results: it was the Christian Church that over many centuries encouraged the abominable and senseless teaching – the teaching of disdain for Jews and Jewishness – which too many times over many centuries had spelled catastrophe for innocents. I believed this was the time to return to my native religion and to act on my decision to become a bridge between Judaism and Christianity. My past and not-forgotten Holocaust experience strengthened feelings of solidarity with my people – with both the murdered and those lucky survivors like myself – and urged me on to work for better understanding between Jews and Christians. Education was the key to success, as I saw it, in this vitally important undertaking for the healing of our world's strife-torn religious factions. I had never forgotten Rabbi Snyder's words and my brief interchange with Augustin Cardinal Bea in Rome. I now felt qualified to become an interpreter of Judaism to Christians, and of Christianity to Jews.

Prior to our departure from Canada, but with Bangor already in the crosshairs, I entered into correspondence with Bangor's Reform Jewish congregation, which happened to be without a rabbi. To my inquiry as to whether they could use a teacher in Judaica subjects, they responded enthusiastically. Shortly after, I also began teaching at Bangor's Jewish Community Center. A bit later still, I founded the Down East Jewish Connection with the help of a Jewish couple who shared my interests. We intended to reach out to Jews in the wider proximity of Bangor to provide education, fun and fellowship.

My time teaching at the Reform Congregation came to a natural end when a rabbinic student from the Reform seminary in Cincinnati arrived. Furthermore, a more conservative approach to Jewish religious practice attracted me in those days, especially an increased use of Hebrew in the services.

Jewish law (Hebrew: *Halakhah*) rules: once a Jew, always a Jew. Even conversion to another religion does not change the religious status of converts in Jewish eyes. *Halakhah* considers that they may have become lapsed or bad Jews, but that they remained Jews. In view of this teaching, my transition to Judaism unfolded easily. At Congregation Beth Israel I told Rabbi Joseph Schonberger my story, answered his questions, and so was reintegrated into the Jewish community. Shortly after, I began studying with him, and before long I became qualified to lead worship services and read Torah, something I enjoyed very much. In addition, I began teaching Yiddish, the Eastern European Jewish language, and the rabbi himself attended my classes. To me, the return to Judaism was exciting and seemed fulfilling.

My father, who had died in 1970, was no longer around to react to my return to Judaism. Just as he was confident in my judgment when I converted to Christianity, he would have said something like this with a reassuring smile: "Walti, I am sure you know what you're doing. I trust your judgment. I wish you luck." My mother probably would have given me a big hug and said, "I love you and trust your decisions. Just remain a decent human being. That's what counts." As for my sister Edith, well, she probably would have said with a smile, "You know what you're doing. *Mazal tov!*" (Yiddish for "good luck").

Sadly, the relationship with my wife gradually worsened. It was clear to me that we could not continue living together. We attempted a trial separation, and Carolyn left to live with Elizabeth, our oldest daughter, in Gainesville, Florida. That situation was not viable.

Carolyn returned home to me, but within a few days, the situation deteriorated even further. She went back to Florida, this time to a retirement community. After a few months there, that arrangement became unacceptable to her. On her request, I purchased a condominium in Bangor for her. She left Florida and settled in there, and we initiated divorce proceedings.

Prior to her absence I met Gail, the woman who became and remains to this day my wife and best friend. And despite several years' silence between Carolyn and me, she and I became friends again. Learning to manage the clinical depression, Carolyn made a new life of her own without me. Amazingly, this included becoming Gail's good friend. Our children and I are deeply grateful for this positive development.

A third important development in Bangor was my involvement as a teacher with Elderhostels that offer learning opportunities for senior citizens. In those days the Elderhostels were organized by colleges and universities. During my last two or three years in Bangor, groups of senior citizens from Florida arrived by bus and participated in Elderhostel courses offered by the university.

Yet a fourth kind of activity which began filling my calendar in those days were my frequent invitations to give courses to middle and high school teachers involved in Holocaust teaching. This educational campaign was organized by the Holocaust and Human Rights Center of Maine in Augusta. My contact with history teachers in these seminars resulted in numerous additional invitations to speak about some of my Holocaust experiences at their and other teachers' schools. School visits, in classrooms as well as at all-school assemblies, have continued to this day. I estimate having reached over forty thousand young people in this manner.

My seven years in Bangor were undoubtedly life-changing. There was sadness – punctuated by the death of my beloved dog Lyla – and there was joy. There were frustrations, and there were accomplishments. But inexorably, the aging process continued, and the severe

## Return to the USA: Bangor, ME, and Weaverville, NC

winter weather of Maine became ever harder to deal with. Gail and I began considering a move to the south of the country, where the climate is more manageable for elderly people. After all, our social security checks would reach us there just as safely as in Maine! Thanks to a family connection of Gail's in Hendersonville, North Carolina, who told us about the beauty and pleasant living conditions of Asheville in western North Carolina, she and I pulled up stakes in Maine and moved to Weaverville, a small town just north of Asheville, in the Appalachian Mountains. The date was 1993.

Weaverville was an excellent choice to let down our anchor. The house we bought was in a section called High Country. It served us well for about five years, after which we moved to another place in town which to this day remains our address. The reasons for the change were multiple. The slope of the lawn was such that I was forced to wear golf shoes while mowing the grass. Also, the steep slope ruled out planting a garden, and I love gardening. The roof-covered deck around half the house kept sunshine out of the living room and one of the bedrooms. I ran out of library space for my many books. Most importantly, opposite our house, a new house in Bavarian style was being built. Once it was finished, it housed a German couple who seemed somewhat older than I. To be honest, this may have been the main motivation for our move. The toxicity left in my system by the Holocaust surfaced then and still comes to the fore every time I meet up with a German person of about my age or older. Such encounters press me to inquire about that German person's occupation during the Holocaust. Was he a soldier, a member of the SS, employed by the *Gestapo*, etc.? Did he perhaps serve in one of the paramilitary groups which in Poland and western Russia hunted down Jews and mass-executed them? The urge is powerful to find out whether that person was a member of the Nazi party. Did he evade the post-World War II denazification process in coming to America? The urge to ascertain his past innocence is powerful. Several times as I was about to ask our neighbor or his wife about their past, my wife discouraged me from doing so, and I desisted. Ursula, one of another pair of elderly German immigrants living a bit farther down the hill, once asked me whether I, also an arrival from Europe, believed all those horror stories being told about concentration camps in which Germans allegedly killed millions of Jews. When I told her that I was a Jew and a survivor of seven such camps, our conversation came to an abrupt halt. "Unbelievable!" was her response as she walked away. We never talked again. Driving by those two homes daily was mentally and, to some extent, even physically so irritating that I felt the need to move away.

Otherwise, our experiences living in Weaverville have been nothing but good. The people here were welcoming and helpful in every way. We enjoy being recognized by the shopkeepers and treated in a friendly manner. As elderly folks, it is extremely important to have access to good medical care. This is certainly the case, both in our little town as well as in nearby Asheville, which has one of the best hospitals in the country.

We consider ourselves very fortunate living in the Appalachian Mountains with their beautiful flora and fauna. Our home is surrounded by rhododendron and azalea bushes, a veritable explosion of color in summertime. Our biweekly drive to the sanitary landfill where we deposit our garbage and trash is a treat, as it winds its way along the French Broad River and offers scenic views along the way. The view from the Blue Ridge Parkway at Mount Pisgah on a clear day is breathtaking, and the food offered in the Pisgah Inn restaurant is delicious. From a culinary standpoint, Asheville and even our little Weaverville are well served. We are proud of the cultural opportunities that Asheville offers. I had the privilege of teaching for several years at the Asheville campus of the University of North Carolina. In our immediate vicinity is Mars Hill University, where I taught my last course as an adjunct professor. Four other colleges are also in the area, and there are sufficient theaters and musical venues to keep one

## Return to the USA: Bangor, ME, and Weaverville, NC

entertained every evening. Last but not least, we are blessed with a pleasant four-season climate. Yes, we chose well in settling here.

In addition to teaching at UNC Asheville and Mars Hill University, I continued teaching with Road Scholar (formerly Elderhostel) under the aegis of the North Carolina Humanities Council. I taught locally as well as along the eastern seaboard (Florida, Georgia, North Carolina, New York, Pennsylvania, Maine) and in Vermont and New Mexico. In association with UNC Asheville, I led a highly appreciated trip to Israel. Here at the town library of Weaverville, I gave several presentations. It was also here that I expanded a course I had taught at UNC Asheville into book form under the title of *The Birth of Christianity from the Matrix of Judaism: From Jewish Sect to World Religion*.

In 2006, I taught a group of B'nai B'rith retired folk at the Chateau Resort and Conference Center in Tannersville in the Pocono Mountains of Pennsylvania. The subject was a comparative religion course dealing with Judaism, Christianity and Islam. The folks were appreciative and said they had learned quite a bit. Great!

For me, the most important thing during that five-day stay took place at the swimming pool. One of the participants, a Jewish woman of German extraction whom I had come to know the previous day, was at the pool also, but we did not talk. I was in the midst of the pool when suddenly to my left I saw this woman drowning. Her head was three or four inches below the water surface; she thrashed around weakly with her arms, and seemed to sink. I must have been the only one in the pool who noticed. Being still a pretty good swimmer even at my advanced age of 79, I quickly swam over and grabbed her under her arm. Paddling with my right arm, I dragged her to the wall of the deep side of the pool where I hung on, holding the woman's head above the water level. I shouted for help. A man sitting by the pool and someone next to me in the water finally helped me get the elderly woman onto a ladder and out of the pool. To make a long story short, the lady was examined by a paramedic of the hotel, and after vomiting a good bit of swallowed water, was laid down on a chaise lounge where she lay immobile for a couple of hours. The next morning at breakfast time, after being informed that it was I who helped her out, she came over and heartily thanked me. The event, in which I played a central role, made me feel good. Among us Jews, it would be said that "I performed a *mitzvah*" – a good deed.

In the next morning's lecture I shared with the participants the Midrash *tehillim* (Book of Psalms) text, the Midrash on Psalm 123:2: "When you are my witnesses, I am God; when you are not my witnesses, I am not God." Then I asked what it meant to be a witness. Among the thirty-plus Jews present there was not one single person who associated the term "witness" with action. How strange! Everyone who spoke could think only of the term "witness" as used in the judicial process of a court of law. They expressed surprise when I explained that witnessing to someone (such as God, for instance) or witnessing to an idea meant "to do" something on behalf of that person or that idea. I asked, "What is love?" and then provided the answer: "Love is something you do." In other words, "witnessing" to the reality of love does not involve merely thinking or meditating about it, but *doing* love. It is downright amazing that my audience, all between sixty and ninety years old, had never been exposed to this idea in their synagogues. This is how deficient some synagogue education is. After the lecture, I had the opportunity to discuss things further with a few folks. "If it had not been for love in action, I, today, would not stand before you," I said, "because had it not been for some individuals in the concentration camps I passed through who 'loved me by doing things for me' – even by jeopardizing their own lives through these acts – I would have died."

In 2009, sixty-two years after immigrating, I returned to my native country, the Czech Republic, accompanied by a faculty colleague from Mars Hill University. I was invited to give the keynote address at a reconciliation conference between Christians and Jews in my

## Return to the USA: Bangor, ME, and Weaverville, NC

hometown in Moravia. On this occasion, a visit to the Jewish cemetery where my grandparents were buried left me shocked. Its overgrown, totally neglected state prompted me to have the shameful situation remedied. A German youth organization, Action Reconciliation Service for Peace, agreed to help clean up the ivy-covered plot, and my request resulted in the organization of a two-week long international youth camp. The cemetery cleanup exposed the work of vandals – broken and displaced tombstones – under the brambles. A plaque with a Czech and English inscription now marks this setting as the last remnant of the town's Jewish community, deported to their death at the concentration camp of Auschwitz on June 29, 1942. It makes me proud to have accomplished this service of respect and love for my Czech Jewish ancestors.

Last but not least, Gail and I found a Jewish congregation, Beth Israel, in Asheville with whom we were able to associate. Shortly after arrival, encouraged by the then rabbi Shmuel (Hebrew for Samuel) Birnham, I became very active teaching and leading worship services. I will never forget the rabbi's calling my arrival here during a worship service "a special blessing sent by God." It is a fact that my coming to Beth Israel resulted in a significant boost in lay members' ability to lead worship services. The recordings I made of the worship leader's singing of the liturgy were used and consulted by a number of our people. This enabled them to step up to worship-related involvement. In appreciation for my services, I was honored with a plaque designating me the "1994-1995 Member of the Year." On May 2, 2010, the congregation honored me with a dinner at the Asheville Country Club that also served as a fundraiser. Proceeds from the 160-guest affair were considerable. I was immensely pleased that all my children and my former wife attended this memorable occasion.

All down here, however, has not been "milk and honey." Difficult challenges came into our lives in the form of serious illness. In the year 2000, during what should have been a lovely vacation in

*Confronting the Silence*

Newfoundland, I came down with pneumonia. The vacation turned into a two-and-a-half week long hospitalization in St. John's, the capital of the island. I fully expected to die. Upon returning home, I was diagnosed with two leukemias that brought me to our excellent local hospital. Thanks to a competent local oncologist, I survived. A few years later, Gail began suffering from cardiac atrial fibrillation. There were several episodes, away from home in hotels, when I thought the end for her had come. The implant of a pacemaker has been a blessing insofar as fibrillation has ceased to occur. This was followed by a gastrointestinal cancer which, thanks to our outstanding medical facilities, was eliminated. Life down here has been good, thanks to the idiosyncrasies of the place itself as well as our good relationships with friends and acquaintances.

Let me conclude this chapter by describing a moment on a camping trip to Prince Edward Island, and the thoughts it engendered in me. The date was July 18, 2006:

> *Gail and I have been camping on Prince Edward Island, one of the Maritime Provinces of Canada. It is beautiful here. We are settled in the Cavendish campground and we live in a tent. It is primitive, of course, but close to nature and that is what we enjoy. The weather has been quite warm and so, come early afternoon, we repair to one of the many beaches in our vicinity and cool off in Mediterranean-like water. Unfortunately there have been jellyfish around. Gail hates them. The slight burning sensation they cause after coming in contact with human skin disappears rather quickly, especially when the spot is rubbed with wet sand.*
>
> *I find myself sitting on the beach and watching the incoming breaking waves. This is very relaxing. But more than that: having recently read Rebecca Goldstein's* Betraying Spinoza,

# Return to the USA: Bangor, ME, and Weaverville, NC

*I find the experience not only relaxing but also in some ways intellectually enlightening. Spinoza's words,* deus sive natura, *God or nature, make a lot of sense to me. In the Hebrew Bible, as also in the* siddur, *the Jewish prayer book, the words* 'ad 'olam, *"for ever," appear again and again. What does eternity mean? How can one get a hold of the concept? Perhaps it is within astronomers' and physicists' grasp, but for me, as a lay person, these are words around which I have not been able to wrap my mind. Theology, which is my field of study, repeatedly uses the term. Mathematics uses the concept of infinity, but can that really be understood? How grasp the notion with our humanly limited minds? Eternity? Infinity?*

*The beach teaches me a lesson. Seeing the ever-repeating process of swells and waves rolling unto the seashore – day after day, year after year, decade after decade, century after century, millennium after millennium, and so on – provides for me an understandable form of the notion of eternity. The incoming wave process never ceases. Countless generations before me experienced the phenomenon and, before humanity came to be, the waves were already there. Is this a notion of eternity? Or, is even this notion insufficient to help us grasp the idea of eternity because, after all, when the sun burns out, the planet as we know it will die, and with it those waves? And then also the notion of eternity and of God will die.*

*I am especially intrigued by the notion of eternity when it comes to texts in the Old Testament. To what extent was the writer of Exodus aware of the real meaning of eternity (infinity of time) when he put the word into the prophet's mouth as God's promise to Israel: "I will be with you forever"? Did the writer of the Book of Samuel understand the notion of infinite time when he had the prophet say to David and later to Solomon, David's son, that God would grant their royal house eternal status? And also, to what extent do my contemporary Jews really believe that Israel as a nation is granted eternal existence? When questioned about this belief, observant Jews (and also Tevye, the Jewish milkman in "Fiddler on the Roof," who proudly proclaims, "We're still here!") point out that many civilizations mentioned in the Bible – the Sumerians, Assyrians, Babylonians and others – no longer exist, whereas the Jews are still here. This is a lame argument. The existence of Israel, when measured from the Sinai event, amounts to a measly three thousand years. What are three thousand years seen against the billions of years of the solar system's and our planet's existence?*

*All this brings me back to Spinoza's* deus sive natura, *God or nature. This is not pantheism, i.e., the notion that God inhabits virtually everything and can therefore be found in everything that exists. As I understand it,* deus sive natura *suggests that it is God who is the organizing principle behind all existence. Whichever name we may assign to this organizing principle, whether it be "All Being," "God," "Ground of Being," or "Nature," it is this reality that created, creates and makes the world go 'round. One could also call this notion "necessity." In the final analysis, however, this is an entity that defies definition. Its essence cannot be determined. It is within this greater scheme that we exist, just like anything else, even the whole universe. In face of this reality one can only be in absolute awe. It is this unnamed entity to which the Talmud writer in the tractate* avodah zarah *refers when he writes, "The world conforms to its natural course." "Natural – nature – natura."*

## Return to the USA: Bangor, ME, and Weaverville, NC

*The Hebrew biblical and post-biblical epithets for this unknowable and inscrutable entity are* Yahweh, Elohim, el shaddai, shekhinah *and others. These represent human attempts to express attributes of this unknowable force in terms of human, limited, totally inadequate language. The genius of certain biblical writers calls attention to our human inadequacy of understanding the god-figure. Isaiah (55:8-9) writes:*

> *---my thoughts are not your thoughts,*
> *neither are your ways my ways, says the LORD.*
> *For as the heavens are higher than the earth,*
> *so are my ways higher than your ways*
> *and my thoughts than your thoughts.*

*Here we have an imagined God speaking imagined words and, interestingly, these are self-correcting words with regard to practically everything the Bible affirms about God elsewhere. This is admirable and exciting.*

*The English word "God," or any other language's expression denoting "God," is a metaphor for the Spinozean birthing, organizing, sustaining, advancing, thrusting, constantly creating and renewing force underlying all and inherent in all that is and ever will be. It resembles, I think, with some modification, what Henri Bergson later called the* élan vital. *This basic energy encompasses all and is impersonal. It is not micromanaging nature or humanity. It follows its self-created trend. A Portuguese proverb states that "God writes straight with crooked lines." I would add in terms of commentary that nature's lines (or call them God's lines, if you prefer) are straight, indeed, inasmuch as they thrust forward in inexorable manner; the crooked lines, on the other hand – human history's lines – are written by us men and women in our circumscribed space-time continuum called planet Earth. The latter are jagged with a lot of ups and downs. They represent our creative positive actions and our failures, and they, too, thrust forward, but in a crooked fashion.*

*Nature is the macro-manager of the universe. In Spinozean terms, this is also called "necessity." The crooked lines mentioned in the Portuguese proverb are something like the pen's writing in a polygraph or EKG machine; the up-and-down squiggles that proceed in a horizontal direction signifying time, represent human action. With our free will, we have enough leeway to operate within that smaller fenced-off area which is ours – the planet Earth – an object in orbit around a star which moves within the same infinite stream of nature's "straight." It is within that "wiggle room," represented by our planet and its potentialities, that the ethical teachings of the Bible, the New Testament, the Quran, the Bhagavad Gita, etc. help us to navigate. These crooked lines must of course be handled and managed responsibly, because it is on these crooked lines that the well-being of the human race depends.*

*Love, goodness, compassion, justice, our human values and virtues, expressed by the word "god" are made real only when we translate them into practice. Traditional Jewish and Christian thinking ascribe these values to God. But the interesting text from Midrash* tehillim *(Book of Psalms), the Midrash on Psalm 123:2, reads, "When you are my witnesses, I am God; when you are not my witnesses, I am not God." This text seems to correct the normative biblical thinking about God. Here it is we who create the "God" of our human* understanding. It is we who bring this self-fashioned "God" into our lives. This "God" is a metaphor for the values that we humans honor and cherish.

It is we who write the "crooked lines" that are so vital for how we human beings live, live together, and let surrounding nature live with us. If we prefer to name this crucial principle of earthly life and the cosmological élan vital by bundling them together into the all-encompassing metaphor "God" – so be it. Ultimately it makes no difference what we call it as long as we DO the ethically right thing here below.

And so after eighty some years, I have figured out our world almost to my satisfaction. Here you have it. You may disagree. That's OK, too. In fact, it is more than just OK! It is the Jewish way. All I want you to do is think things over with me!

Isn't it amazing, though, that after all this cogitation, I sometimes still catch myself praying to the lieber Gott of my good mother when I thought to have definitively dethroned Him.

Go figure!

# EPILOGUE
# New Horizons

I find myself to have been richly blessed. Notice that the preceding sentence does not end with the usual formula, "blessed by God." You, the reader of these lines, may wonder why the omission of the word "God." This must be intentional, you think, to which I respond with, "Yes, it is intentional."

I initially entitled this memoir *In Search of God*. In retrospect, I believe my life has been just such a search, both within my soul and professionally – the latter through my research and writing. At this point in my life, I have ceased searching because I have found not God, evidently, but a truth that has a liberating effect on me and the way I am conducting my life. I must confess, however, that at times I feel sad to have lost the childlike faith of my youth, as I already mentioned elsewhere. This is what I now want to explain in conclusion.

With Nicolaus Copernicus' (1473-1543) formulation of the heliocentric model of our planetary system, the biblically acquired belief that the earth and humanity are at the center of the universe, both physically and in the sense of ultimate importance, came to an end. The 2004 NASA Cassini mission to the planet Saturn provided us with a photograph of planet Earth, taken by its camera then located close to the rings of the planet, which shows our earth as a luminous dot among a multitude of other such dots. Astronomers tell us that we are one among fifteen billion trillion other stars and planets out there in space.

When Charles Darwin (1809-1882) formulated the Theory of Evolution, the biblical idea of the creation of humans, as presented in the Genesis creation narrative, came crashing down. With the process of natural selection now firmly established as scientific fact, and thanks also to magnificent developments in biology, chemistry, medicine and other fields, evolution can no longer be referred to pejoratively as being "only a theory." Einstein's Theory of Relativity also opened our eyes to a new understanding of the universe, and in so doing revolutionized the fields of physics, astrophysics, and astronomy.

Whether or not the Big Bang Theory, which tries to explain the origin of our universe, is correct, I do not know. But whether correct or incorrect, it strikes me as more cogent than the biblical account of creation. The scientific enterprise has vastly enlarged and enriched our understanding of the cosmos, on both the micro and macro levels. I am deeply grateful to the scientific giants who advanced our comprehension of the universe.

Science-based insights have led me to discard my belief in the biblical God. My personal experience of the Holocaust undoubtedly deepened my disenchantment with the whole biblical God idea. "Where was God at Auschwitz?" also became my personal whispered cry. The phrase contains sadness, disappointment, but also accusation. One of the important admonitions attributed to the biblical God is found in the Book of Leviticus 19:16. According to our Jewish sages it reads in translation from the Hebrew, "You shall not stand idly by the blood of your neighbor." Bystanders to a human catastrophe are, in Jewish eyes, just as guilty as the perpetrators of the catastrophe themselves. This brings me back to the Holocaust and the murder of six million Jews, my co-religionists, my brothers and sisters in the faith. During that disaster there were human onlookers and bystanders

## EPILOGUE: New Horizons

galore. But who, I ask, was the supposed most powerful bystander of all who did not move even one little finger to stop that human butchery? Clearly it was the God who violated his own precept, the alleged originator of the biblical command, "You shall not stand idly by the blood of your neighbor." Supreme scandal! And so, even if the biblical God were a reality, his passivity during this and many other human and nature-caused mass tragedies prevents me from adoring, worshiping and following him. This being said, I am relieved that this rather shamefully acting God does not exist and never did.

This means that my "Search for God" has ended. I agree with Epicurus (341-270 B.C.) and his wise words heard long ago in Professor Stumpf's philosophy class at Vanderbilt:

*Is God willing to prevent evil, but not able?*
*Then he is not omnipotent.*
*Is he able but not willing?*
*Then he is malevolent.*
*Is he both able and willing?*
*Then whence cometh evil?*
*Is he neither able nor willing?*
*Then why call him God?*

Now what about "religion"? Where do I stand there? The term "religion" derives from the Latin *religare*, to bind, to connect. Its usage over the ages clearly pertains to the binding or connection of humans to God and vice versa. Clearly, this biblically taught mutual relationship is based on the premise that there is such a one as God. But once the truth of this premise turns out to be erroneous, the notion of a God-human-God relationship falls into the category of mere human assumption. No God – no religion!

My return to Judaism was replete with hope of having "come home," in the words of the good Rabbi Snyder, and of my having found God and all that this implies in terms of happiness, security, joy, fulfillment and mission. In the process of studying theology and surveying Jewish and general history, I found that religion's major affirmations about God are wrong. Eventually I was no longer able to read, let alone believe, Jewish prayer book texts such as "Praised are you, LORD, our God and God of our fathers, the great, strong and awesome God, the God of Abraham, the God of Isaac and the God of Jacob, etc." This is the introductory statement to the *Amidah*, the all-important standing prayer, recited three times daily. The truth is that by and large the whole Jewish liturgy is based on the foundational Exodus event which describes the Jewish slaves' liberation from Egypt, a highly mythologized narrative. I ask, what about Jewish history – the millennia of documented Jewish suffering – since the Exodus? Did the God of the biblical narratives actually intervene? The great, strong and awesome God? What about that overwhelming silence from above?

It follows for me that with God's reality invalidated by science and documented history, the prayer book recitations of religious myths no longer hold because they are a non-sense. I refuse to recite non-sense in a liturgical setting, pretending that I believe what I recite.

This brings me back to good ol' Epicurus, whose wisdom, for me, prevails because it does make sense. None of the Jewish or Christian priests, prophets, scholars and holy men succeeded, despite their intellectual somersaults in trying to preserve the notion of an almighty and all-good God who acts in history. I raise my glass to Epicurus, a truly wise man, who saw the truth and proclaimed it.

Do I find any good in the notion of religion and its practice? Yes, I do, to some extent, in that it creates community. Community is beneficial to human beings. None of us wants to live alone, in isolation from fellow human beings, devoid of support in difficult times and without fellow celebrants in good times. But I ask, cannot community form and operate on principles other than non-sense?

## EPILOGUE: New Horizons

A load has been taken off my shoulders. I believe in the power of what human common sense and good can accomplish. I have become a Jewish secular humanist. Some of my coreligionists on the extreme right of the theological spectrum, and also some Christian readers, might find it impossible to be a Jew and a non-believer. So let me explain. Already in the *Yerushalmi*, the Jerusalem Talmud (including *Mishna*, compiled by 400 C.E.), in the tractate *Chagigah* ("festival offerings"; chapter 1:7), we read the following saying attributed to God: "Would that they forsake Me but keep My Torah." This text suggests that the God of Judaism subordinates Himself to the Torah. Before I continue, let me explain that the term *torah*, always translated in the New Testament as "law," really means instruction, guidance or law, depending on the term's literary context. Other similar texts could be cited. So, what does Jewish secular humanism mean to me? It means that having eliminated the superstitious biblical God-idea, I do subscribe to many of the eternal values of Judaism and of Christianity, Judaism's daughter/sister religion. Let me make it clear, however, that in choosing those Jewish biblical and rabbinic values which I admire and accept for my daily living, I use the best critical thinking I am capable of. My choices are not arbitrary ones, but rather those which, in my opinion, contribute to the well-being of the world in which I live and thus also affect my person. In Judaism this kind of thinking and action is called *tikkun olam* or "healing/repair of the world."

But let me add in a whispered voice that at times it saddens me to have lost my simple childlike faith, which made daily life easier, safer feeling and more optimistic.

It depresses me to see that so many people in our world are reluctant or unable to use common sense. It seems as if human greed and insatiable desire to dominate "the other" control human behavior. I choose to call this destructive attitude – evil.

As I contemplate our world, I see good and evil in constant competition. If one adds to the inclination of evil the attribute of ignorance, the result of the mix is deadly. Education, in my opinion, is the only possible remedy to overcome this supreme human dilemma.

Let me end with two recent experiences that symbolize, as it were, what I have tried to say above. Walking into our bank in Weaverville the other day, I passed a young man leaving the building. He was over six feet tall and strongly built. The man wore a sleeveless T-shirt. A quick glance at him revealed on one shoulder the tattoo of a swastika, the emblem of the Nazis, and on the other, that of the murderous Nazi paramilitary organization, the SS. The young man never saw me, I am sure, but I saw him, and what I saw sent shivers down my spine. Part of me wanted to stop and ask him what these two symbols meant to him. But even if all this had not happened so fast, I doubt that I would have had the courage to do so. I measure only five foot five – enough said. Two symbols of pure evil tattooed in his skin.

Following one of my visits to a middle school where I shared my Holocaust experiences, I received a box in the mail. In that box were 116 letters addressed to me, each in a separate envelope. It took me several hours to open and read these notes of thanks, some brief, some much longer. One of the letters came from a child named Laura. Like others, she expressed her thanks to me for coming and sharing, and then she continued with, "I want you to know, Walter, that had I lived then, I gladly would have given my life, had I known that this act could prevent the suffering and death of so many innocent people of all ages." I sat there stunned as I read these lines. Tears came to my eyes. Tears of gratitude. With youngsters like these, despite their obvious naiveté, there is still hope, I said to myself.

Before us lie choices – death or life. The ideology of the young man with the tattoos represents death. The heartfelt attitude expressed by the little girl in one written line represents hope and life.

I vote for Laura – for hope and life.

# BIOGRAPHICAL TIMELINE FOR WALTER ZIFFER

| 1927 | Born in Cieszyn (Poland). Moves to Český Těšín (Czechoslovakia) a couple of days later. |
|---|---|
| 1938 | Poland annexes the Zaolzie (Polish: trans-Olza River) territory. The Ziffers become Poles. |
| 1939 | Nazis occupy Český Těšín. |
| 1942 | The Ziffers are deported to Sosnowitz. Walter is later transferred to the following slave-labor camps: Sakrau, Brande, Gräditz, Nimptsch, Klettendorf, Schmiedeberg, and Waldenburg / Gross-Rosen. |
| 1945 | Liberated by Soviet army in Waldenburg/Gross-Rosen concentration camp. Repatriates to Český Těšín. |
| 1947 | Departs for Paris and Champigny-sur-Marne (suburb of Paris). |
| 1948 | Immigrates to the United States and arrives in Nashville, Tennessee. |
| 1949 | Enrolls in Hume-Fogg Technical and Vocational High School. |
| 1950 | Graduates from Hume-Fogg and enrolls in Vanderbilt University. |
| 1951 | Converts to Christianity (Church of Christ). |
| 1953 | Marries Carolyn Harris Kinnard. |
| 1954 | First child, Elizabeth, born. |
| 1954 | Graduates from Vanderbilt University with Bachelor of Science in Engineering. |
| 1954 | Begins employment with the Inland Manufacturing Division of General Motors Corporation in Dayton, Ohio. Earns five U.S. patents during the next five years. |
| 1956 | Second child, Deborah, born. |
| 1958 | Third child, Ruth, born. |

| | |
|---|---|
| 1960 | Leaves General Motors. Enrolls in Graduate School of Theology (GST) of Oberlin College, Ohio. |
| 1961 | Fourth child, Timothy, born. |
| 1963 | Graduates from Oberlin's GST with Master of Arts in New Testament and Greek. |
| 1964 | Receives Master of Theology from GST in Biblical Studies (Old Testament and Hebrew). |
| 1964 | Moves to Le Chambon-sur-Lignon, France, as Co-Director (with Carolyn) of *Accueil Fraternel* |
| 1969 | Moves to Montpellier, France, as guest professor at *Faculté de Théologie Protestante* |
| 1970 | Walter's father, Leo (Tati), dies in Havířov, Czech Republic. |
| 1971 | Graduates from *l'Université de Strasbourg* with Doctor of Theology degree. |
| 1972 | Moves to Washington, DC as pastor of the Concordia United Church of Christ. Also joins the faculty of the Inter-faith Metropolitan theological seminary. |
| 1977 | Moves to Brussels, Belgium, to serve as pastor of the American Protestant Church. |
| 1982 | Retires to Kempt, Queens County, Nova Scotia, Canada. |
| 1987 | Moves to Orrington, Maine. Teaches as adjunct professor at the University of Maine in Orono. |
| 1987 | Returns to Judaism. Joins Congregation Beth Israel, Bangor, Maine. |
| 1990 | Publishes *The Teaching of Disdain: An Examination of Christology and New Testament Attitudes Toward Jews*. |
| 1991 | Divorced from Carolyn Kinnard Ziffer. |
| 1992 | Travels to Europe with Gail Rosenthal. Introduces Gail to his mother, Anny Ziffer. |
| 1993 | Walter's mother Anny (Mutti) dies in Havířov, Czech Republic. |
| 1993 | Moves to Weaverville, North Carolina. |

| | |
|---|---|
| 1994 | Teaches as adjunct professor in the Classics Department at the University of North Carolina at Asheville. Teaches at Elderhostels in and out of state. Becomes Research Professor for Jewish Studies at UNC Asheville (UNCA). |
| 1995 | Recognized as Member of the Year at Congregation Beth Israel, Asheville, North Carolina. |
| 1999 | Marries Gail R. Rosenthal. |
| 1999 | *The Birth of Christianity from the Matrix of Judaism* used for instruction at UNCA. |
| 2000 | Recovers from pneumonia and leukemia (chemotherapy at Mission Hospital, Asheville). |
| 2001 | Teaches as adjunct professor at Mars Hill College (now Mars Hill University), Mars Hill, North Carolina. |
| 2002 | Sister, Edith, dies in Havířov, Czech Republic. |
| 2006 | Receives "Tzadik" (righteous one) plaque of appreciation from Mars Hill College |
| 2006 | *The Birth of Christianity from the Matrix of Judaism* published by AuthorHouse in a revised edition. |
| 2007 | Receives plaque of appreciation from the North Carolina Center for the Advancement of Teaching, Cullowhee, North Carolina. |
| 2009 | Keynote speaker at Czech *Konference Smíření* (Conference of Reconciliation/Atonement), Český Těšín, Czech Republic. |
| 2009 | Discovers overgrown Jewish cemetery in Český Těšín and spearheads 2010 cleanup by a German youth organization, Action Reconciliation Service for Peace. |
| 2015 | Memorial plaque with Czech and English inscriptions manufactured in Asheville, NC and installed at Jewish cemetery in Český Těšín. |
| 2015 | Retires from regular teaching at Mars Hill University. |
| Ongoing | Lectures on invitation through the North Carolina Humanities Council and by private invitation at various educational venues. |

# FOR FURTHER READING:

Christopher Browning. *Ordinary Men: Reserve Battalion 101 and the Final Solution in Poland*. New York: Aaron Asher Books/HarperCollins Publishers, 1992.

John G. Gager. *The Origins of Anti-Semitism: Attitudes Toward Judaism in Pagan and Christian Antiquity*. Revised edition. Oxford: Oxford University Press, 1985.

Daniel Jonah Goldhagen. *Hitler's Willing Executioners*. New York: Alfred A. Knopf, 1996.

Philip Hallie. *Lest Innocent Blood Be Shed: The Story of the Village of Le Chambon and How Goodness Happened There*. New York: Harper & Row, 1979.

Raul Hilberg. *The Destruction of the European Jews*. Second edition, 3 volumes. New York: Holmes & Meier, 1985.

Walter Laqueur. *The Changing Face of Anti-Semitism: From Ancient Times to the Present Day*. Oxford: Oxford University Press, 2006.

Rosemary Radford Ruether. *Faith and Fratricide: The Theological Roots of Anti- Semitism*. New York: The Seabury Press, 1974.

Gabriel Schoenfeld. *The Return of Anti-Semitism*. San Francisco: Encounter Books, 2004. Also available as an e-book, published 2006.

Elie Wiesel. *Night*. New York: Hill and Wang, 2006. Translated from the Yiddish by Marion Wiesel. Includes preface to the new translation and Nobel Prize acceptance speech. Originally published in 1958 by Les Éditions de Minuit, France, as *La Nuit*. First published in the United States by Hill and Wang, 1960.

Simon Wiesenthal. *The Sunflower: On the Possibilities and Limits of Forgiveness*. Revised and expanded edition. New York: Schocken Books, 1998. Translation of *Die Sonnenblume*, originally published in 1970 by Hoffmann and Campe, in Hamburg, Germany.

# DISCUSSION QUESTIONS

1. What word(s) would you use to describe Walter's family life before WW II (chapters 1 – 3)? How did his experiences as a child prepare him (or not) for what came later in his life?

2. Based on the Holocaust section of Walter's memoir (chapters 4 – 11), how would you describe the evolution of his personality? Did his character have anything to do with how or why he survived?

3. Based on the same section of this memoir, how do you think the author would describe human nature? (Be specific: refer to the text.) Now that you have added the experience of this book to your own understanding, how would you describe human nature?

4. What aftereffects did Walter experience from his imprisonment as a teenager? How did imprisonment change his family life before he left for America (chapters 10 – 13)?

5. Walter describes several post-war experiences with German, Czech, and Polish people. Why do you think he reacted negatively sometimes, and sometimes positively?

6. What were Walter's reasons (plural...!) for converting to Christianity and eventually becoming a Christian minister (chapters 14 – 15)? Do you believe that they are valid? Why or why not?

7. What was the impact on Walter of Elie Wiesel's book *Night* (chapter 16)? Why do you think it was so important to him?

8. In the latter part of his memoir, Walter discusses his late-in-life return to Judaism (chapters 19 – 20). Compare and contrast Walter's practice of Judaism with that of his father.

9. What has been the role of education in Walter's life? What value does he put on education for himself and for others?

10. What experiences in your own life are illuminated by Walter's story? What would you tell him in a letter about your own personal history as it relates to his?

# THE WILMA DYKEMAN LEGACY

**WILMA DYKEMAN (1920-2006)** was a native of Asheville, North Carolina. From her parents, who read to each other in the evenings, Wilma inherited her love of literature. Their books connected them to the world. "From this little mountain cove," Wilma later wrote, "we could reach out across space and time to know strange people and places and the intertwined evil and good that awaited our innocence and our choices." These were the memories that influenced her life's path of writing, giving speeches, and traveling the world.

Wilma was eternally curious, an independent thinker, and a strong and confident woman who often tackled controversial subjects. In her novels, she wrote about mountain people, their personalities, their lives and struggles in Appalachia. She dismantled the stereotype of Appalachians being backward and uneducated, instead portraying them as proud, independent, and resourceful.

Wilma broke new ground in the fields of environmental conservation (1955), oral history (1950's), civil rights (1957), Appalachian Studies (1960's), chemically altered foods (1973), birth control (1974), and women's rights (throughout her life). She argued that a clean environment benefits the economy, and that the way we treat our environment reflects the way we treat other people. "As we have diminished one whole segment of our people," she wrote in *Neither Black Nor White* in 1957, "we have diminished ourselves."

The Dykeman Legacy Press is the imprint of the Wilma Dykeman Legacy, a non-profit tax exempt charity dedicated to sustaining Wilma Dykeman's core values of environmental integrity, social justice, and the power of the written and spoken word. The Wilma Dykeman Legacy is proud to publish Walter Ziffer's memoir as a spur to social justice, and for its documentary power.

Visit www.wilmadykemanlegacy.org for more information.

**PUBLISHING COMMITTEE OF THE WILMA DYKEMAN LEGACY:**

Sharon Fahrer
Terry Roberts
Elaine Smyth
Jim Stokely

**FOUNDING CONTRIBUTORS TO THE WILMA DYKEMAN LEGACY:**

Rosemary Armstrong and Sandy Weinberg
Randy and Lynn Stokely
Morris Weinberg, Sr.

**ADDITIONAL CURRENT AND FORMER MEMBERS OF
THE BOARD OF DIRECTORS OF THE WILMA DYKEMAN LEGACY:**

Karen Cragnolin
Mimi Fenton
Johnnie Grant
Darin Waters
James Abbott
Deborah Miles
Robert Neufeld
Jesse Ray, Jr.
Robert Riddle
Dianne Tuttle
Helen Wykle

www.ingramcontent.com/pod-product-compliance
Lightning Source LLC
Chambersburg PA
CBHW070422010526
44118CB00014B/1862